"Discover the limitless potential of computer science and engineering with this accessible and comprehensive guide, tailored specifically for non-CSE Enthusiasts looking to gain a deeper understanding of the intricate world of technology."

INTRODUCTION TO COMPUTER SYSTEMS AND SOFTWARE ENGINEERING

COMPUTER SCIENCE ENGINEERING (CSE) FOR NON-CSE ENTHUSIASTS

ENAMUL HAQUE

Last update: July 2024
Published: March 2023

ISBN: 978-1-4477-9056-3
Imprint: lulu.com

Publisher:
ENEL PUBLICATIONS
London, United Kingdom
Cover Photo by Andrea Piacquadio[i]

- THE STORY BEHIND THIS BOOK –

Once upon a time, a young person had always been fascinated by technology and computers but never had the chance to learn about them in depth. They wanted to explore the exciting world of Computer Science Engineering but were intimidated by the technical jargon and the complex concepts.

That's when they stumbled upon a book that promised to demystify the world of Computer Science Engineering for non-technical students. The book claims to provide a comprehensive overview of everything one needs to know about computer systems and software engineering in a language that anyone can understand.

Excited by the prospect of finally understanding the mysteries of technology, the young person bought the book and started reading. As they delved deeper into the pages, they discovered a treasure trove of information about computer systems, programming languages, software engineering, app development, and more.

They learned about the history of computers, the components of a computer system, and the different types of computer software. They discovered the principles of programming languages and how to design and develop their own apps without technical knowledge. They even learned about emerging technologies like Artificial Intelligence, IoT, and Blockchain and how they are shaping the future of computing.

With every turn of the page, the young person felt more and more empowered and excited about their newfound knowledge. They felt like they were finally part of the world of technology and couldn't wait to explore it further.

Suppose you are a non-technical student who is always curious about computer science and engineering. In that case, this book is the perfect guide to help you discover the wonders of this exciting field. With its easy-to-understand language and comprehensive coverage of all the essential topics, this book will transform you from a curious outsider to a confident insider in no time.
So why wait? Get your copy today and start exploring the exciting world of Computer Science Engineering!

ENEL PUBLICATIONS
London, United Kingdom
Revision 01 – July 2024

CONTENTS

INTRODUCTION

So, a warm welcome to "Computer Science Engineering (CSE) for Non-CSE Enthusiasts: Introduction to Computer Systems and Software Engineering."

This book is designed to introduce non-computer science engineering students to the fundamental concepts of computer systems and software engineering. Computer systems have become ubiquitous today, and software engineering has become an essential aspect of almost every field. This book aims to provide a comprehensive overview of computer systems and software engineering principles and practices, enabling students to understand and work with them more effectively.

The book is divided into three chapters: "Introduction to Computer Systems", Introduction to Programming" and "Introduction to Software Engineering." In the first chapter, you will learn about the history of computers, the components of a computer system, computer hardware, software, operating systems, computer networks, cloud computing, edge computing, usability, and interaction. The second chapter will deal with all sorts of things on computer programming. In the third chapter, you will learn about the definition and objectives of software engineering, the characteristics of good software, the comparison with other engineering disciplines, computer system engineering, programming languages, object-oriented programming, software design process, and an introduction to programming.

This book is ideal for students who do not have a background in computer science engineering but are interested in learning about computer systems and software engineering. The book assumes no prior computer science or programming knowledge and is written in a simple and accessible language. The book also includes practice questions and answers, exercises, and projects to reinforce the concepts learned.

I hope this book will be a helpful resource for students seeking a solid understanding of computer systems and software engineering. Let's get started!

OTHER BOOKS FOR NON-CSE ENTHUSIASTS

This book is the first volume of a series on Computer Science Engineering (CSE) for non-CSE Enthusiasts. In addition to this book, I am working on releasing two more volumes covering Mathematics for Computing, Algorithms and Data Structures, Skills Required for the Digital Age, Trends in Computer Science, Digital Literacy and the Future of Computing.

On Algorithms and Data Structures, covering sorting and searching algorithms, data structures like arrays, linked lists, stacks, queues, trees, and graphs, and algorithm analysis techniques like dynamic programming and greedy algorithms.

Skills Required for the Digital Age include analytical and problem-solving skills, critical thinking and creativity, programming skills, data structures and algorithms skills, basic web development knowledge, basics of machine learning, security, vulnerabilities, and cryptography, time management and continuous learning, interdisciplinary knowledge, and communication skills.

Trends in Computer Science, including data science, artificial intelligence, machine learning, the Internet of Things (IoT), virtualisation, computer simulation, robotics, image processing, cybersecurity, information-driven entrepreneurship and enterprise, DevOps, blockchain, quantum computing, augmented and virtual reality, and natural language processing.

Another focus is Digital Literacy, covering topics like digital communication, online safety and security, information literacy, digital citizenship, digital tools and platforms, user experience design, big data, human-computer interaction, digital ethics, and data visualisation.

The topic on the Future of Computing, including emerging technologies and trends, ethical considerations in computing, the social and cultural impact of computing, sustainability and green computing, challenges and opportunities in computing, and preparing for the future of computing.

WHO IS THIS BOOK FOR?

This book, "Computer Science and Engineering (CSE) for Non-CSE Enthusiasts," is primarily intended for students interested in gaining a foundational understanding of computer science and engineering but may not have a background in CSE. It is designed for students in their first year of university or who have completed their A-levels with a background in a non-CSE field, such as ICT.

The book is also useful for professionals looking to expand their computer science and engineering knowledge to help them succeed. For example, someone in marketing or finance may benefit from a better understanding of data analytics or cybersecurity.

This book is written for anyone who wants to learn computer science and engineering fundamentals and see how they apply them to other disciplines. The book is written in a way that makes the principles discussed in each chapter easy to learn and implement by providing a range of activities, examples, and case studies.

WHAT WILL YOU LEARN IN THIS BOOK?

In "Computer Science and Engineering (CSE) for Non-CSE Enthusiasts," readers will learn a broad range of topics related to computer science and engineering, including:

- The basics of computer systems, including their history, components, architectures, and use cases.
- The different types of computer hardware and how they work together, including basic input/output system (BIOS) and its tasks.

- The various types of computer software, including system, application, programming, and utility software, and how they are used.
- Operating systems' basic concepts and functions include process and memory management, file systems, storage management, security, and protection.
- The basics of computer networking, including the types of networks, devices, topologies, and protocols, and network security and cryptography.
- The basics of cloud computing and edge computing, including their deployment models, benefits and drawbacks, and use cases.
- The basics of user-centred design, human-computer interactions (HCI), usability testing and evaluation, and user experience (UX) design.
- The fundamental concepts of software engineering, including its definition, objectives, evolution, and characteristics of good software, and the software design process.
- A computer system's components include operating systems and system software, application software, distributed systems and networking, robotics and cybernetics, embedded systems, computer graphics and visualization, medical image computing (MIC), computer and network security, database management system, and emerging technologies.
- The overview of programming languages, including imperative, object-oriented, functional, scripting, and markup languages, and object-oriented programming concepts, such as classes and objects, inheritance and polymorphism, and encapsulation and abstraction.

WHAT IS THE NEXT SERIES WOULD INCLDUE

- Various programming algorithms and data structures, including sorting and searching algorithms, arrays, linked lists, stacks, queues, trees, graphs, algorithm analysis, dynamic programming, and greedy algorithms.
- The soft and technical skills required for the digital age, including analytical and problem-solving skills, critical thinking and creativity, programming skills, data structures and algorithms skills, basic web development knowledge, basics of machine learning, basics of security, vulnerabilities, and cryptography, time management and continuous learning, interdisciplinary knowledge and communication skills.
- Current computer science trends include data science, artificial intelligence, machine learning, IoT, virtualisation, computer simulation, robotics, image processing, cybersecurity, information-driven entrepreneurship and enterprise, DevOps, blockchain, quantum computing, augmented and virtual reality, and natural language processing.
- The concepts of digital literacy include digital communication, online safety and security, information literacy, digital citizenship, digital tools and platforms, user experience design, big data, human-computer interaction, digital ethics, and data visualisation.
- The future of computing, including emerging technologies and trends, ethical considerations in computing, the social and cultural impact of computing, sustainability and green computing, challenges and opportunities in computing, and how to prepare for the future of computing.

Throughout the book, readers will also be able to engage with practical exercises, examples, and case studies that demonstrate the practical applications of the concepts covered in each chapter. By the end of this book, readers will have gained a broad understanding of computer science and engineering. They will be well-equipped to apply this knowledge in their academic and professional pursuits.

INTRODUCTION TO COMPUTER SYSTEMS

INTRODUCTION TO COMPUTER SYSTEMS

Have you ever wondered how your computer works? A computer system comprises hardware and software components that enable computing. In this chapter, we will explore the key elements of a computer system and its role in enabling modern computing.

One of the essential components of a computer system is the CPU, which stands for the central processing unit. The CPU is responsible for performing calculations and running programs on your computer. It's like the "brain" of the computer!

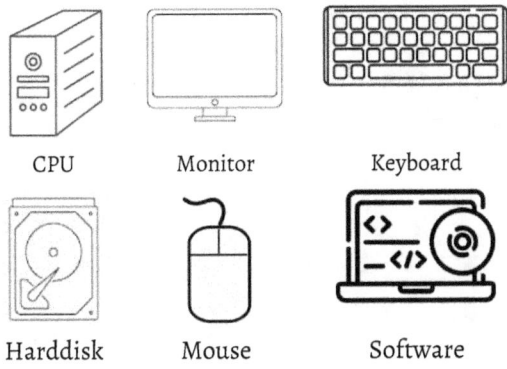

| CPU | Monitor | Keyboard |
| Harddisk | Mouse | Software |

Figure 1 - Computer parts

Another essential component of a computer system is memory, which stores information that the CPU is currently working with. There are different types of memory, including RAM and cache memory, which we will learn more about in later chapters.

In addition to the CPU and memory, a computer system also includes storage devices, such as hard drives and solid-state drives, which are used to store data and programs even when the computer is turned off.

Input/output devices, like your keyboard, mouse, and monitor, are used to interact with the computer and receive information from it. This is how you see what's happening on your computer screen and input information into programs.

We'll also learn about computer architectures and systems, including personal computers, mainframes, supercomputers, and embedded systems. Each of these systems has its own unique features and use cases.

The information presented in the Introduction to Computer Systems chapter should equip you with a solid grounding in the fundamentals of what makes up a computer system and how they interact to make modern computing possible. You'll need this background info to make it through the next few chapters, which will expand on this knowledge to discuss more sophisticated CSE concepts.

HISTORY OF COMPUTERS

The history of computers dates back several centuries, with early devices used for calculating and record-keeping. Some earliest examples include the abacus, the astrolabe, and the slide rule. These were all mechanical devices that used physical mechanisms to perform calculations.

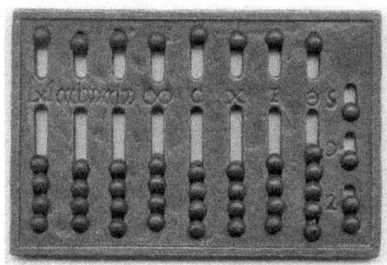

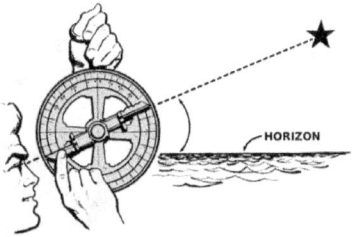

Figure 2 - A Roman abacus[2]   *Figure 3 - Line art drawing of an astrolabe[3]*

In the 19th century, Charles Babbage designed the Difference and Analytical engines, which were early mechanical computers. However, neither of these machines was ever completed during Babbage's lifetime.

The first electronic computers were developed in the mid-20th century, starting with the Colossus machine used by the British during World War II to break encrypted German communications. Harvard Mark I, ENIAC, and other early electronic computers followed this.

Throughout the 1950s and 1960s, the development of computers continued, with the introduction of magnetic storage, high-level programming languages, and the first operating systems. In the 1950s and 1960s, computers became more sophisticated and were used for various applications, including scientific research, military operations, and business applications. The development of integrated circuits in the mid-1960s led to the development of smaller and more powerful computers used in various fields, including space exploration, medical research, and financial analysis.

In the 1970s, the first personal computers, including the Apple II and the Commodore PET, were introduced. This led to the widespread adoption of computers in homes and businesses.

In the 1980s and 1990s, computer hardware continued to evolve, introducing faster processors, larger memory capacities, and graphical user interfaces. The Internet also emerged during this time, connecting computers and users worldwide.

Figure 4 - Analytical Engine by Charles Babbage[4]

In the 21st century, computers have become ubiquitous, with billions of devices in use worldwide. They continue to evolve, with advancements in artificial intelligence, cloud computing, and other technologies shaping the future of computing.

WHAT IS A COMPUTER SYSTEM?

A computer system comprises hardware and software components that perform various computing tasks. The hardware components include the central processing unit (CPU), memory, storage devices, input/output devices, and other peripheral devices. The software components include the operating system and various applications that run on the computer system.

The CPU is the "brain" of the computer and is responsible for performing arithmetic and logical operations, executing instructions, and controlling data flow within the computer system. The memory stores data and instructions that the CPU needs to access quickly. The storage devices, such as hard disk drives and solid-state drives, store data and programs even when the computer is turned off. Input/output devices, such as keyboards, mice, monitors, and printers, allow users to interact with and receive information from the computer system.

The software components include the operating system, which manages the computer's resources and provides a platform for other applications to run on. Other applications, such as web browsers, productivity software, and games, provide users with a wide range of functionality and allow them to perform various tasks on the computer system.

A computer system is a sophisticated collection of hardware and software that cooperates to make contemporary computing possible.

COMPONENTS OF A COMPUTER SYSTEM

The components of a computer system include:

Central Processing Unit (CPU): The CPU is the "brain" of the computer system and is responsible for executing instructions and performing calculations. It consists of an arithmetic logic unit (ALU) and a control unit

(CU) and is designed to carry out operations on data stored in memory or input by users.

Memory: Memory is the area of the computer where data and instructions are stored. There are different types of memory, including Random Access Memory (RAM), which is volatile and loses its data when the computer is turned off, and Read-Only Memory (ROM), which is non-volatile and retains its data even when the computer is turned off.

Figure 5 - Components of a computer system

Storage devices: Storage devices are used to store data and programs on the computer system. Examples of storage devices include hard disk drives (HDD), solid-state drives (SSD), and USB flash drives.

Input/Output (I/O) devices: I/O devices allow users to interact with the computer system and receive information from it. Examples of I/O devices include keyboards, mice, monitors, printers, scanners, and speakers.

Together, these components work together to enable modern computing. The CPU retrieves instructions and data from memory and performs operations on them. Memory stores data and instructions that are currently in use. Storage devices store data and programs even when the computer is turned off. I/O devices allow users to input information and receive output from the computer system.

COMPUTER ARCHITECTURES AND SYSTEMS

Computer architectures and systems refer to different computer systems with unique features, designs, and use cases. There are several types of computer architectures and systems, including:

Figure 6 - IBM mainframe computer[5]

Personal computers (PCs): Personal computers are designed for individual use and come in different forms, including desktops, laptops, and tablets. They are typically used for general-purpose computing, such as web browsing, productivity applications, and gaming.

In addition to these types of computer architectures and systems, there are also different types of computer networks, such as Local Area Networks (LANs) and Wide Area Networks (WANs), which enable communication between different computers and devices.

Understanding the different types of computer architectures and systems is essential for understanding each type's unique features, strengths, and weaknesses and how they are used in various industries and applications.

USE CASES

Computer systems: Computer systems are used in a wide range of industries and applications, including:

- Healthcare: Electronic health records, telemedicine, and medical imaging all rely on computer systems to manage patient data and enable remote care.
- Finance: Trading platforms, banking applications, and risk analysis all rely on computer systems to process transactions and provide real-time data analysis.
- Education: Learning management systems, e-learning platforms, and educational software all rely on computer systems to manage course content and facilitate student learning.

Components of a computer system:

- CPU: The CPU is used in various applications, including video encoding, scientific simulations, and gaming.
- Memory: Memory stores data and instructions that the CPU needs to access quickly. This includes running multiple applications simultaneously and switching between them quickly.
- Storage devices: Storage devices are used to store data and programs. This includes personal files, documents, media files, and software.

- Input/Output (I/O) devices: I/O devices are used for inputting data and outputting information. This includes peripherals like keyboards, mice, and printers.

Computer architectures and systems:
- Personal computers (PCs): PCs are used for general-purpose computing tasks like web browsing, productivity, and entertainment.
- Mainframes: Mainframes are used in industries that require high-volume transaction processing, like banking, finance, and government agencies.
- Supercomputers: Supercomputers are used in scientific and engineering fields for tasks like climate modelling, drug design, and aerospace engineering.
- Embedded systems: Embedded systems are used in devices like smart home technology, automotive electronics, and medical devices.

EXERCISES

These exercises can help individuals deepen their understanding of computer systems, components, and architectures and help them develop a more comprehensive understanding of how these technologies are used in various industries and applications.

Computer systems:
- Research and report on how computer systems are used in a specific industry, such as healthcare, finance, or education.
- List five applications or programs that you regularly use on your computer system. For each application, describe the program's primary function and how it relies on computer systems to function.

Components of a computer system:

- Research and report on the different types of memory used in computer systems, including their advantages and disadvantages.
- Create a diagram of a computer system and label the CPU, memory, storage devices, and input/output devices.

Computer architectures and systems:
- Research and report on the different types of computer networks, including their advantages and disadvantages.
- Compare and contrast the features and use cases of personal computers, mainframes, supercomputers, and embedded systems.

KEY TAKEAWAYS

- A computer system comprises hardware and software components that work together to process and manage data.
- The CPU is the brain of the computer system, responsible for executing instructions and performing calculations.
- Memory is the area where data and instructions are stored. There are different types of memory, including volatile and non-volatile memory.
- Storage devices are used to store data and programs on the computer system. Examples of storage devices include hard disk drives, solid-state drives, and USB flash drives.
- Input/output (I/O) devices allow users to interact with and receive information from the computer system. Examples of I/O devices include keyboards, mice, monitors, printers, and scanners.
- Graphics processing units (GPUs) are specialised hardware components designed to perform complex calculations and render images and graphics.
- Network interface cards (NICs) allow computers to connect to a network and communicate with other devices.

- The motherboard is the main circuit board of a computer system, connecting all the hardware components together.
- The power supply unit (PSU) provides power to the computer system, converting AC power from an electrical outlet into DC power that the computer's components can use.
- Understanding the different hardware components of a computer system is essential to troubleshoot problems, upgrading parts, and building or repairing a computer system.

EXERCISE ANSWERS

Computer systems:

Research and report on how computer systems are used in a specific industry, such as healthcare, finance, or education.

Acceptable answer: For example, in the healthcare industry, computer systems manage patient data, including electronic health records and medical imaging. These systems also facilitate telemedicine, allowing patients to receive remote care from medical professionals.

List five applications or programs that you regularly use on your computer system. For each application, describe the program's primary function and how it relies on computer systems to function.

Acceptable answer: For example, one application that I use regularly is a web browser. The web browser relies on computer systems to download and render web pages and store and manage user data, such as bookmarks and browsing history. The primary function of the web browser is to allow me to access and view websites on the Internet.

Components of a computer system:

Research and report on the different types of memory used in computer systems, including their advantages and disadvantages.

Acceptable answer: For example, two main types of memory are used in computer systems: volatile and non-volatile. Volatile memory, such as RAM, stores data that the CPU needs to access quickly. The advantage of volatile memory is its speed, but the disadvantage is that it loses its data when the computer is turned off. Non-volatile memory, such as ROM and flash memory, is used for storing data that needs to be retained even when the computer is turned off. The advantage of non-volatile memory is its persistence, but the disadvantage is that it is slower than volatile memory.

Create a diagram of a computer system and label the CPU, memory, storage devices, and input/output devices.

Acceptable answer: A diagram of a computer system should include a CPU, memory, storage devices, and input/output devices, all interconnected by a bus. The CPU should be labelled as the computer's " brain, " while the memory should be labelled as the "working area" of the CPU. The storage devices should be labelled as the "long-term memory" for the computer, and the input/output devices should be labelled as the "senses" and "effectors" of the computer.

Computer architectures and systems:

Research and report on the different types of computer networks, including their advantages and disadvantages.

Acceptable answer: For example, there are several types of computer networks, including Local Area Networks (LANs), Wide Area Networks (WANs), and Wireless Networks. LANs connect devices in a single location, such as a home or office, while WANs connect devices across large distances, such as different cities or countries. Wireless networks use radio waves to connect devices without the need for physical cables. The advantages of computer networks include improved communication, resource sharing, and remote access, while the disadvantages include security risks, maintenance costs, and technical complexity.

Compare and contrast the features and use cases of personal computers, mainframes, supercomputers, and embedded systems.

Acceptable answer: Personal computers are used for general-purpose computing tasks, such as web browsing, productivity, and entertainment. Mainframes are used in industries that require high-volume transaction processing, such as banking, finance, and government agencies. Supercomputers are used in scientific and engineering fields for climate modelling, drug design, and aerospace engineering tasks. Embedded systems are used in smart home technology, automotive electronics, and medical devices. Each of these systems has its own unique features, strengths, and weaknesses and is designed for specific use cases.

COMPUTER HARDWARE

Computer hardware refers to the physical components of a computer system, including the devices that make up the computer and allow it to function. These include the central processing unit (CPU), memory, storage devices, input/output (I/O) devices, and other peripheral devices.

TYPES OF COMPUTER HARDWARE

CPU: The CPU is the "brain" of the computer system and is responsible for executing instructions and performing calculations.

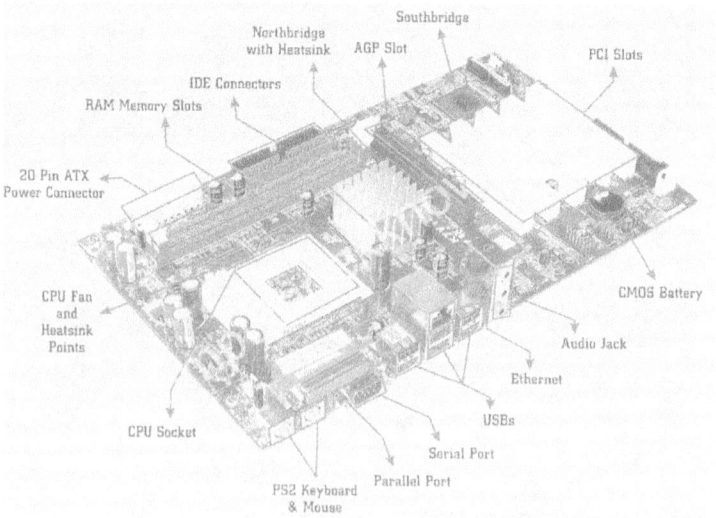

Figure 7 - Computer motherboard components

Memory: Memory is the area of the computer where data and instructions are stored. There are different types of memory, including Random Access Memory (RAM), which is volatile and loses its data when the computer is turned off, and Read-Only Memory (ROM), which is non-volatile and retains its data even when the computer is turned off.

Storage devices: Storage devices are used to store data and programs on the computer system. Examples of storage devices include hard disk drives (HDD), solid-state drives (SSD), and USB flash drives.

Input/Output (I/O) devices: I/O devices allow users to interact with the computer system and receive information from it. Examples of I/O devices include keyboards, mice, monitors, printers, scanners, and speakers.

Graphics processing units (GPUs): GPUs are specialised hardware components that are designed to perform complex calculations and render images and graphics. They are commonly used in gaming and multimedia applications and scientific and engineering simulations.

Network interface cards (NICs): NICs are hardware components that allow computers to connect to a network and communicate with other devices. They typically provide an Ethernet or Wi-Fi interface and support various network protocols.

Motherboard: The motherboard is the main circuit board of a computer system, which connects all the hardware components together. It contains the CPU, memory, other components, and expansion slots for additional hardware.

Power supply unit (PSU): The PSU is a hardware component that provides power to the computer system. It converts AC power from an electrical outlet into DC power that the computer's components can use.

Sound cards: Sound cards are used to process and output audio signals, enabling a computer to produce sound.

Cooling systems: Cooling systems, such as fans or liquid cooling, are used to dissipate heat generated by the CPU and other components to prevent overheating.

Peripherals: Peripherals are external devices that connect to a computer system, such as cameras, microphones, and external hard drives.

Expansion cards: Expansion cards are hardware components that can be added to a computer system to provide additional functionality or enhance performance, such as graphics cards, sound cards, or network interface cards.

System buses: System buses are the communication pathways that connect a computer system's CPU, memory, and other components. They can be internal, connecting components within the same computer, or external, connecting components across different systems.

BIOS/UEFI firmware: BIOS/UEFI firmware is a program stored on the motherboard that initialises and configures the computer hardware during startup.

Chipsets: Chipsets are collections of electronic components that work together to manage the flow of data between the CPU, memory, and other components of a computer system.

Battery backup: Battery backup systems provide uninterrupted power to a computer system in the event of a power outage or other electrical disruptions.

HOW HARDWARE COMPONENTS WORK TOGETHER

The hardware components of a computer system work together in a complex process to perform computing tasks. The CPU retrieves instructions and data from memory and performs operations on them. Memory stores data and instructions that are currently in use. Storage devices store data and programs even when the computer is turned off. I/O devices allow users to input information and receive output from the computer system. Together, these components enable modern computing.

Let's say you want to open a document on your computer. When you click on the document icon, the I/O device (such as the mouse or keyboard) sends a signal to the CPU, which retrieves the instruction to open the document from memory. The CPU then sends a signal to the storage device (such as the hard drive) to retrieve the document data and load it into memory. Once the data is loaded into memory, the CPU performs operations on it, such as rendering the text and graphics and sending the output to the I/O device (such as the monitor) to display the document on the screen. As you type or make changes to the document, the I/O device sends signals to the CPU, which retrieves the new data from memory and performs operations on it, updating the display on the screen in real-time. Once you save and close the document, the CPU sends a signal to the storage device to write the data back to the storage device for future use.

COMPUTER AND ASSEMBLY LANGUAGE

A computer system is a study of how the hardware components of a computer system are structured and how they work together to process information. This includes topics such as computer architecture, instruction set design, memory systems, and input/output systems.

A critical aspect of a computer is the instruction set architecture (ISA), which defines the set of instructions that a CPU can execute. The ISA includes instructions for performing arithmetic and logical operations, memory access, and input/output operations. Assembly language is a low-level programming language that uses mnemonics to represent these instructions in a more human-readable format. Assembly language is used to write programs that the CPU can directly execute, bypassing the need for a compiler or interpreter.

Assembly language is often used in systems programming, device driver development, and other low-level tasks where performance and hardware control are important. Assembly language is typically more difficult to write and read than higher-level programming languages like Java or Python. However, it provides more control over the hardware and can be more efficient for certain types of applications.

In addition to assembly language, a computer also encompasses topics such as memory systems, input/output systems, and computer architecture. Memory systems include the different types of memory used in a computer system, such as cache, RAM, and ROM. Input/output systems include the devices used to interact with the computer system, such as keyboards, mice, and monitors.

Computer architecture refers to a computer system's overall structure and design, including the number and type of processors, the memory and storage, and the interconnects between components.

Computer and assembly language are important topics for computer science and engineering students to understand. They provide a deeper understanding of how computer systems work and how to program them at a low level.

BASIC INPUT/OUTPUT SYSTEM (BIOS)

A Basic Input/Output System (BIOS) is typically written in assembly language, although some portions may also be written in C or other languages. BIOS is a firmware program that is stored in non-volatile memory on a computer's motherboard and is responsible for initialising and configuring the computer's hardware components during the boot process.

Since BIOS operates at a very low level and needs to interact directly with the hardware, it is typically written in assembly language to provide maximum control and efficiency over the system. Assembly language allows the BIOS to directly access the CPU, memory, and other hardware components, and it can provide more fine-grained control over system initialisation and configuration. However, writing and debugging assembly code is more difficult and time-consuming than using a higher-level language, so some portions of BIOS may be written in higher-level languages to simplify development and maintenance.

In addition to initialising and configuring hardware components, the BIOS also performs various self-tests to ensure the system functions properly. These self-tests are called Power-On Self Tests (POST), and they check the system's hardware components for errors and faults. If the BIOS detects any errors during the POST, it will generate error messages and stop the boot process, preventing the system from starting up.

The BIOS also provides a basic set of input/output services, known as BIOS interrupts, that the operating system uses to communicate with the hardware. These interrupts allow the operating system to access low-level hardware features, such as the hard disk drive and video display and provide a standard interface for hardware communication.

In modern computers, the BIOS has mainly been replaced by a newer technology called Unified Extensible Firmware Interface (UEFI). UEFI provides more advanced features and capabilities than the traditional BIOS, such as support for larger hard drives, faster boot times, and improved security. However, UEFI still performs many of the same functions as the BIOS, such as hardware initialisation and configuration.

TASKS PERFORMED BY BIOS

Power-On Self-Test (POST): When a computer is turned on, the BIOS runs a series of checks called the Power-On Self-Test (POST) to make sure that all the hardware components are functioning properly. This includes checking the CPU, memory, storage devices, and I/O devices. If any errors are detected during the POST, the BIOS will usually display an error message or beep code to alert the user.

Booting the operating system: After the POST is complete, the BIOS loads the operating system into memory and hands control over to the operating system. The BIOS reads the boot loader code from the hard drive or other bootable device and executes it to load the operating system. The BIOS also sets up the system's memory map, interrupt handlers, and other system-level settings that are required by the operating system.

Configuring hardware settings: The BIOS provides a user interface for configuring various hardware settings, such as the system clock, boot order, and hardware resources. These settings can be accessed through the BIOS setup utility, which is usually accessed by pressing a key (such as F2 or Del) during the boot process. The BIOS setup utility allows the user to configure the system to their specific needs and preferences.

Updating BIOS firmware: The BIOS firmware can be updated to fix bugs, improve performance, or add new features. BIOS updates are usually provided by the computer manufacturer and can be installed by downloading the firmware update file and running it from within the operating system or from a bootable USB drive.

BIOS is a critical computer system component responsible for initialising and configuring the hardware components during the boot process. The computer could not boot up and load the operating system without the BIOS.

USE CASES

Automotive: Hardware components like sensors, processors, and communication modules are used in vehicles to enable advanced driver-assistance systems (ADAS), navigation, and entertainment.

Manufacturing: Industrial hardware components like programmable logic controllers (PLCs), sensors, and robotics are used to automate manufacturing processes and improve efficiency.

Aerospace: Hardware components like avionics systems, control systems, and flight simulators are used in the aerospace industry for flight control, navigation, and pilot training.

Home Automation: Hardware components like smart thermostats, smart lights, and home security systems are used to automate and control various aspects of the home environment.

Retail: Hardware components like point-of-sale (POS) systems, scanners, and digital displays are used in the retail industry to process transactions and provide customer information.

EXERCISES

- *Identify and describe the components of a motherboard:* In this exercise, students can be asked to research and describe the various components of a motherboard, including the CPU socket, RAM slots, expansion slots, power connectors, and other components.

- *Build a computer:* This exercise involves having students build a computer from scratch using various hardware components. They will need to choose compatible components, assemble them, and install the operating system and drivers.

- *Troubleshooting hardware issues:* In this exercise, students can be presented with various hardware issues, such as a computer that won't turn on, a printer that won't print, or a monitor that displays distorted images. They will need to diagnose the issue and suggest possible solutions.

- *Hardware compatibility:* In this exercise, students can be given a list of hardware components and asked to determine if they are compatible with each other. This will require them to research specifications and understand how different components work together.

- ***Upgrade a computer:*** This exercise involves having students upgrade an existing computer by replacing or adding hardware components, such as RAM, a new graphics card, or a larger hard drive. They will need to research compatible components and follow proper installation procedures.

KEY TAKEAWAYS

- The CPU is the "brain" of the computer system and is responsible for executing instructions and performing calculations.
- Memory is where data and instructions are stored, including RAM and ROM.
- Storage devices like hard disk drives (HDD), solid-state drives (SSD), and USB flash drives store data and programs.
- Input/output (I/O) devices like keyboards, mice, monitors, printers, scanners, and speakers allow users to interact with the computer system.
- Graphics processing units (GPUs) are specialised hardware components in gaming, multimedia applications, and scientific/engineering simulations.
- Network interface cards (NICs) allow computers to connect to a network and communicate with other devices.
- The motherboard is the main circuit board of a computer system that connects all the hardware components together.
- The power supply unit (PSU) provides power to the computer system and converts AC power to DC power.
- The computer system is the study of how the hardware components of a computer system are structured and how they work together to process information.
- Assembly language is a low-level programming language that uses mnemonics to represent CPU instructions in a more human-readable format.

EXERCISE ANSWERS

Identify and describe the components of a motherboard:

The components of a motherboard include the CPU socket, RAM slots, expansion slots, power connectors, BIOS chips, CMOS battery, chipset, and various other connectors and ports.

Build a computer:

To build a computer from scratch, students must choose compatible components, such as a CPU, motherboard, RAM, storage device, power supply, and case. They will need to assemble these components and install the operating system and drivers.

Troubleshooting hardware issues:

To troubleshoot hardware issues, students will need to diagnose the problem, such as checking for loose connections or testing the hardware components. They will need to suggest possible solutions, such as updating drivers or replacing faulty components.

Hardware compatibility:

To determine hardware compatibility, students must research the components' specifications and understand how different components work together. They will need to check for factors such as socket type, form factor, and power requirements.

Upgrade a computer:

To upgrade a computer, students will need to research compatible components, such as RAM, a new graphics card, or a larger hard drive. They will need to follow proper installation procedures, such as shutting down the computer, disconnecting the power supply, and handling the components carefully.

COMPUTER SOFTWARE

Computer software refers to a set of instructions or programs that tell a computer what to do. It is a collection of computer programs, procedures, and documentation that perform tasks on a computer system. There are many different types of software, including systems, applications, programming, and utility software.

Figure 8 - Different software

SYSTEM SOFTWARE

This type of software is responsible for managing the hardware components of a computer system and providing a platform for running other software applications. Examples of system software include operating systems (such as Windows, macOS, and Linux), device drivers, firmware, and system utilities.

APPLICATION SOFTWARE

This type of software is designed to perform specific tasks or applications, such as word processing, spreadsheet management, web browsing, or image editing. Examples of application software include Microsoft Word, Adobe Photoshop, Google Chrome, and QuickBooks.

PROGRAMMING SOFTWARE

This type of software is designed for developers and programmers to write, test, and debug computer code. Examples of programming software include compilers, debuggers, and integrated development environments (IDEs).

UTILITY SOFTWARE

This type of software is designed to perform various system maintenance and management tasks, such as disk cleanup, data backup, system optimisation, and virus protection. Examples of utility software include antivirus software, system optimisers, backup software, and disk defragmentation tools.

COMPILER

A compiler is a software tool that translates source code written in a programming language into an executable program that can be run on a computer. It inputs the entire source code and translates it into machine code that the computer can understand. Examples of popular compilers include GCC (GNU Compiler Collection) for C and C++ and Java Compiler for Java.

In addition to GCC and Java Compiler, there are several other popular compilers used in the industry, including:

Clang: Clang is an open-source C/C++/Objective-C compiler used to build high-performance applications.

Visual C++ Compiler: The Visual C++ Compiler is a proprietary compiler part of Microsoft's Visual Studio development environment.

Intel C++ Compiler: The Intel C++ Compiler is a commercial compiler designed to optimise applications for Intel processors.

LLVM Compiler: The LLVM Compiler is a modular compiler infrastructure used to build high-performance compilers for a wide range of programming languages.

Use cases of compilers include:

Application development: Compilers are commonly used in software development to convert source code into machine code that can be executed on a computer.

Gaming: Compilers develop high-performance games that can run on various platforms.

Scientific computing: Compilers are used to develop applications for scientific computing, such as simulations, data analysis, and machine learning.

Operating system development: Compilers are used to develop operating systems like Linux and macOS.

Embedded systems: Compilers develop software for embedded systems, such as microcontrollers and IoT devices.

Compilers play a critical role in software development by converting source code into machine code that can be executed on a computer, allowing developers to create high-performance applications for various use cases.

INTERPRETERS

An interpreter is a software tool that executes the source code of a program directly without the need for compilation. It reads and executes the code line by line, interpreting each instruction as it goes. Interpreters are commonly used for scripting languages like Python and JavaScript, where developers can quickly prototype and test code.

Interpreters are commonly used in web development for client-side scriptings, such as JavaScript, where the browser interprets the code. They are also used in server-side scriptings, such as PHP and Ruby on Rails, where the server interprets the code.

One of the advantages of using an interpreter is that it allows for quick prototyping and testing of code, as the code can be executed immediately without the need for compilation. It also allows for greater flexibility, as code can be modified on-the-fly and errors can be fixed more quickly.

Examples of popular interpreters include Python Interpreter for Python, Node.js for JavaScript, and Ruby Interpreter for Ruby. Use cases for interpreters involve developing web applications, scientific computing, and automation scripts.

ANTIVIRUS AND MALWARE

Antivirus and malware software is designed to protect computers from malicious software that can harm, disrupt or destroy data on a computer. Antivirus software works by scanning files and looking for patterns of code that match known viruses and malware. It then either removes or quarantines the malicious code. Examples of popular antivirus software include Norton, McAfee, and Avast. On the other hand, malware is a type of software designed to harm or disrupt computer systems. Examples of malware include viruses, worms, and Trojan horses. Anti-malware software is specifically designed to detect and remove malware from computer systems. Examples of popular anti-malware software include Malwarebytes and Spybot Search and Destroy.

Antivirus and malware software has become increasingly important as the Internet has become more integrated into our daily lives. Some additional use cases for antivirus and malware software include:

Protection against phishing attacks: Phishing is a type of social engineering attack that involves tricking users into divulging sensitive information, such as usernames and passwords, through fraudulent websites or emails. Some antivirus software includes anti-phishing features that can help users identify and avoid these attacks.

Protection against ransomware: Ransomware is a type of malware that encrypts a victim's files and demands payment in exchange for the decryption key. Some antivirus software includes ransomware protection features that can detect and block ransomware attacks before they can do any damage.

Protection for mobile devices: As more and more people use mobile devices like smartphones and tablets to access the Internet, antivirus and malware software for mobile devices has become increasingly important. Some popular antivirus software for mobile devices includes Avast Mobile Security and Norton Mobile Security.

Protection for home networks: Some antivirus software also includes features that can help protect home networks from attacks, such as firewalls and network monitoring tools. These features can help prevent unauthorised access to home networks and block attacks before they can do any damage.

Antivirus and malware software is essential for protecting computer systems and data from various threats. As new threats continue to emerge, these tools will evolve to provide even better user protection.

SOFTWARE USE CASES

Productivity software: These types of software are used by businesses and individuals to streamline their work and increase productivity. Examples include Microsoft Office, Google Docs, and Trello.

Creative software: Artists, designers, and musicians use these types of software to create digital content. Examples include Adobe Creative Suite, ProTools, and Blender.

Educational software: These types of software are used in classrooms and other educational settings to enhance learning. Examples include Moodle, Khan Academy, and Rosetta Stone.

Financial software: These types of software are used by businesses and individuals to manage finances, track expenses, and make financial decisions. Examples include QuickBooks, TurboTax, and Mint.

Gaming software: These types of software are used for gaming and entertainment purposes. Examples include Steam, Xbox Live, and PlayStation Network.

Communication software: These types of software are used to facilitate communication between individuals and groups. Examples include Slack, Zoom, and Skype.

Security software: These types of software are used to protect computer systems from threats like viruses and malware. Examples include Norton, McAfee, and Avast.

EXERCISES

- Research and describe the differences between system software and application software. Give examples of each and explain how they work together.
- Choose an application software program, such as Microsoft Word or Adobe Photoshop. Research and describe the different features and capabilities of the program. Then, create a short tutorial on how to use one of the features.
- Research and describe the different types of programming software, including compilers, debuggers, and integrated

development environments (IDEs). Choose one type of programming software and create a short presentation on its features and capabilities.

- Choose a popular utility software program, such as antivirus software or system optimiser. Research and describe the different features and capabilities of the program. Then, create a short tutorial on how to use one of the features.

- Research and describe the differences between interpreters and compilers. Give examples of each and explain how they are used in software development. Then, create a short presentation on the advantages and disadvantages of each method.

KEY TAKEAWAYS

- System software manages the hardware components of a computer system, while application software performs specific tasks or applications.

- Examples of system software include operating systems, device drivers, firmware, and system utilities.

- Examples of application software include Microsoft Word, Adobe Photoshop, Google Chrome, and QuickBooks.

- Programming software includes compilers, debuggers, and integrated development environments (IDEs).

- Utility software performs various system maintenance and management tasks, such as disk cleanup, data backup, system optimisation, and virus protection.

- Microsoft Word is an application software program used for word processing, document creation, and editing.

- Developers and programmers use programming software to write, test, and debug computer code.

- Antivirus software is a type of utility software that scans for and removes or quarantines malicious code.

- Interpreters execute the source code of a program directly without the need for compilation, while compilers translate source code into machine code that can be executed on a computer.
- Understanding the different types of software and their features and capabilities is essential for computer users and developers alike.

EXERCISE ANSWERS

Differences between System and Application Software:

System software manages computer hardware and provides a platform for running other software applications. It includes operating systems (such as Windows, macOS, and Linux), device drivers, firmware, and system utilities. On the other hand, application software is designed to perform specific tasks or applications, such as word processing, spreadsheet management, web browsing, or image editing. Examples of application software include Microsoft Word, Adobe Photoshop, Google Chrome, and QuickBooks.

System and application software work together using system resources like CPU, memory, and storage to perform tasks. Application software relies on system software to access hardware resources like input/output devices and network connections. For example, Microsoft Word relies on the operating system to access the printer to print a document.

Tutorial on Application Software:

For this exercise, students can choose a popular application software program like Microsoft Word or Adobe Photoshop. They can research the different features and capabilities of the program and choose one feature to create a short tutorial. For example, a tutorial on how to use the "Track Changes" feature in Microsoft Word can be created, which includes step-by-step instructions and screenshots.

Presentation on Programming Software:

Students can research and describe the different types of programming software, including compilers, debuggers, and integrated development environments (IDEs). Then they can choose one type of programming software and create a short presentation on its features and capabilities. For example, a presentation on an IDE like Visual Studio can be created, which includes information on its debugging tools, code editing features, and project management capabilities.

Tutorial on Utility Software:

Students can choose a popular utility software program like antivirus software or system optimisers for this exercise. They can research the different features and capabilities of the program and choose one feature to create a short tutorial. For example, a tutorial on performing a system scan using Malwarebytes antivirus software can be created, including step-by-step instructions and screenshots.

Presentation on Interpreters and Compilers:

Students can research and describe the differences between interpreters and compilers, give examples of each, and explain how they are used in software development. Then, they can create a short presentation on the advantages and disadvantages of each method. For example, a presentation that compares the speed of compiled code versus interpreted code and the flexibility of interpreted code versus compiled code can be created.

OPERATING SYSTEMS

Operating systems (OS) are essential components of modern computer systems. The OS manages the computer's CPU, memory, storage, and input/output devices. An operating system is a program that manages the hardware resources of a computer and provides a platform for running other applications.

Figure 9 - Different operating systems

BASIC CONCEPTS AND FUNCTIONS OF OPERATING SYSTEMS

Operating systems perform various functions, including managing resources, providing a user interface, running applications, and providing security and protection. Some basic concepts and functions of operating systems include:

Kernel: The core component of the operating system that manages system resources and provides services to other programs. Examples include the Windows NT kernel in Microsoft Windows and the Linux kernel in Linux distributions.

User interface: The interface through which users interact with the operating system and applications. Examples include the graphical user interface (GUI) used in Windows and macOS and the command line interface (CLI) used in Linux.

System calls: Interfaces that allow applications to request services from the operating system. Examples include the fopen() function in C, which requests the opening of a file, and the read() function, which requests the reading of data from a file.

Multi-tasking: The ability of the operating system to run multiple programs at the same time. Examples include the ability to have multiple windows open in a web browser or multiple programs running simultaneously on a computer.

PROCESS MANAGEMENT AND SCHEDULING

Operating systems manage processes, which are instances of programs that are executing on the system. Process management and scheduling involve allocating resources to processes and determining which process to run at a given time. The operating system uses scheduling algorithms to decide which process should run next and for how long. Examples of process management and scheduling include the task manager in Windows, which displays information about running processes and allows users to end them, and the Linux process scheduler, which uses the Completely Fair Scheduler (CFS) algorithm to allocate CPU resources to processes.

MEMORY MANAGEMENT AND VIRTUAL MEMORY

Memory management is the process of allocating and deallocating memory to programs. The operating system manages the memory to ensure that programs can access the memory they need and prevent memory conflicts. Virtual memory is technique operating systems use to expand the amount of memory available to programs. It allows programs to use more memory than is physically available by temporarily storing data on the hard drive.

Examples of memory management and virtual memory include using paging and swapping in Windows and Linux, which move data between RAM and the hard drive to free up memory and using memory-mapped files, which map files on disk to virtual memory addresses.

FILE SYSTEMS AND STORAGE MANAGEMENT

Operating systems manage storage devices and provide a file system that allows users to organise and access files. The file system provides a hierarchical structure for organising files and directories, and the operating system provides tools for managing files and storage devices. Examples of file systems and storage management include the FAT32 and NTFS file systems used in Windows, the ext4 file system used in Linux, and the Disk Utility tool in macOS, which allows users to partition and format storage devices.

SECURITY AND PROTECTION

Operating systems provide security and protection features to prevent unauthorised access and protect the system and user data. This includes authentication and authorisation mechanisms, access control policies, encryption and decryption, and antivirus and firewall software. Examples of security and protection features include the Windows Security Center, which provides a centralised location for managing security settings and antivirus software, and the Linux iptables firewall, which provides network security by filtering network traffic.

Examples of security and protection features in operating systems include:

Authentication and authorisation mechanisms: These features ensure that only authorised users can access the system and its resources. Examples include login passwords, biometric authentication, and smart cards.

Access control policies: These features define the permissions and privileges that users and programs have on the system. Examples include user roles, file permissions, and security groups.

Encryption and decryption: These features protect data from unauthorised access by encrypting it before it is stored or transmitted. Examples include BitLocker and EFS in Windows and LUKS and dm-crypt in Linux.

Antivirus and firewall software: These features protect the system from viruses, malware, and other malicious software. Examples include Windows Defender and McAfee in Windows, ClamAV, and Firestarter in Linux.

Secure boot: This feature ensures that the operating system is loaded securely and has not been modified by malware or other malicious software. Examples include UEFI Secure Boot in Windows and Linux.

OPERATING SYSTEM SOFTWARE

Operating system (OS) software is a program that manages computer hardware and software resources and provides common services for computer programs. It acts as an interface between the user and the computer hardware, allowing users to interact with the computer and run applications.

The key functions of an operating system include process management, memory management, device management, file management, and security. Process management involves scheduling and running multiple tasks or programs simultaneously. Memory management is responsible for allocating and deallocating memory to different programs. Device management involves controlling the use of input and output devices such as printers, keyboards, and monitors. File management is responsible for organising and controlling access to files and directories. Security involves protecting the system and its data from unauthorised access, viruses, and other threats.

Operating systems can be categorised into several types based on their architecture, such as batch processing systems, real-time systems, network operating systems, and desktop operating systems. Each type of operating system has different design and performance considerations, and the choice of the operating system depends on the user's or 's specific needs and requirements.

An operating system is a fundamental computer system component responsible for managing hardware and software resources, providing common services for computer programs, and allowing users to interact with the computer.

Some of the very common operating systems are:

Windows - Developed by Microsoft, Windows is a popular operating system used in personal computers. It has a user-friendly interface and supports a wide range of software and hardware.

macOS - Developed by Apple, macOS is the operating system used in Apple computers. It has a sleek interface and is known for its stability and security.

Linux - Linux is an open-source operating system that is popular in servers and embedded systems. It is highly customisable and supports a wide range of software and hardware.

Android - Developed by Google, Android is a popular operating system used in smartphones and tablets. It is based on the Linux kernel and supports many apps and services.

iOS - Developed by Apple, iOS is the operating system used on iPhones and iPads. It is known for its stability, security, and user-friendly interface.

Chrome OS - Developed by Google, Chrome OS is a lightweight operating system designed for use in Chromebooks. It is highly optimised for web browsing and supports various web-based apps.

Unix - Unix is a family of operating systems that is popular in servers and workstations. It is highly customisable and is known for its stability, security, and scalability.

These are just a few examples of the many available operating systems. Each operating system has its own strengths and weaknesses, and the choice of the operating system depends on the user's specific needs and requirements.

EXERCISES

1. Define the kernel of an operating system and explain its role in managing system resources.
2. Describe the difference between the graphical user interface (GUI) and the command line interface (CLI) used in operating systems. Provide examples of each.
3. Explain the concept of virtual memory and how it is used in operating systems. Provide examples of operating systems that use virtual memory.
4. Discuss the purpose and importance of file systems in operating systems. Provide examples of file systems used in popular operating systems.
5. Describe operating systems' security and protection features and provide examples of software tools used to protect systems from viruses, malware, and other security threats.

KEY TAKEAWAYS

- Operating systems are essential components of modern computer systems that manage hardware resources and provide a platform for running other applications.
- The core component of the operating system is the kernel which manages system resources and provides services to other programs.

- Operating systems perform various functions, including managing resources, providing a user interface, running applications, and providing security and protection.
- Process management and scheduling involve allocating resources to processes and determining which method to run at a given time.
- Memory management allocates and deallocates memory to programs, and virtual memory is a technique used to expand the amount of memory available to programs.
- Operating systems manage storage devices and provide a file system that allows users to organise and access files.
- Security and protection features in operating systems include authentication and authorisation mechanisms, access control policies, encryption and decryption, antivirus and firewall software, and secure boot.
- Some examples of common operating systems are Windows, macOS, Linux, Android, iOS, Chrome OS, and Unix.
- Each operating system has its own strengths and weaknesses, and the choice of the operating system depends on the user's specific needs and requirements.
- Understanding operating systems' basic concepts and functions can help non-CSE students better understand how computers work and how to use different software applications effectively.

EXERCISE ANSWERS

1. Operating systems (OS) manage the computer's CPU, memory, storage, and input/output devices. An OS is a program that addresses the hardware resources of a computer and provides a platform for running other applications. System software includes the operating system, device drivers, and utility programs. Application software includes programs designed for specific tasks, such as word processing, spreadsheets, and web browsers.

2. The kernel is the core component of the operating system that manages system resources and provides services to other programs. Examples include the Windows NT kernel in Microsoft Windows and the Linux kernel in Linux distributions. The user interface is the interface through which users interact with the operating system and applications. Examples include the graphical user interface (GUI) used in Windows and macOS and the command line interface (CLI) used in Linux. System calls are interfaces that allow applications to request services from the operating system. Examples include the fopen() function in C, which requests the opening of a file, and the read() function, which requests the reading of data from a file. Multi-tasking is the ability of the operating system to run multiple programs at the same time. Examples include having multiple windows open in a web browser or multiple programs running simultaneously on a computer.

3. Process management and scheduling involve allocating resources to processes and determining which process to run at a given time. The operating system uses scheduling algorithms to decide which process should run next and for how long. Examples of process management and scheduling include the task manager in Windows, which displays information about running processes and allows users to end them, and the Linux process scheduler, which uses the Completely Fair Scheduler (CFS) algorithm to allocate CPU resources to processes.

4. Virtual memory is technique operating systems use to expand the amount of memory available to programs. It allows programs to use more memory than is physically available by temporarily storing data on the hard drive. Memory management is the process of allocating and deallocating memory to programs. The operating system manages the memory to ensure that programs can access the necessary memory and prevent memory conflicts. Examples of memory management and virtual memory include

using paging and swapping in Windows and Linux, which move data between RAM and the hard drive to free up memory and using memory-mapped files, which map files on disk to virtual memory addresses.

5. Operating systems manage storage devices and provide a file system that allows users to organise and access files. The file system provides a hierarchical structure for organising files and directories, and the operating system provides tools for managing files and storage devices. Examples of file systems and storage management include the FAT32 and NTFS file systems used in Windows, the ext4 file system used in Linux, and the Disk Utility tool in macOS, which allows users to partition and format storage devices.

COMPUTER NETWORKS

Computer networking is the practice of connecting computers and other devices to share resources and communicate with each other. Some of the basic concepts and topics related to computer networking include:

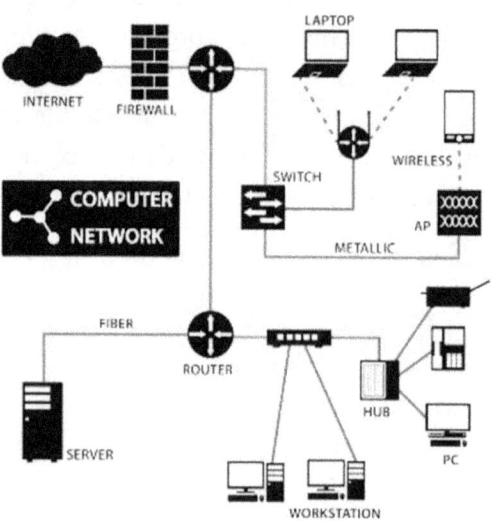

Figure 10 - Computer network

BASICS OF COMPUTER NETWORKING

The basics of computer networking refer to the concepts and principles of how computers communicate over a network. A computer network is a collection of interconnected devices, such as computers, servers, routers, switches, and other devices, that can share resources and communicate with each other.

A network protocol is a set of rules governing how data is transmitted over the network. The basic components of a computer network include nodes, which are the devices that are connected to the network, and the communication links that connect them. The links may be wired or wireless, depending on the type of network.

Networking involves several layers of abstraction, including the physical, data link, network, transport, and application layers. Each layer has a specific function and services the layers above and below. For example, the physical layer transmits raw data over the network, while the transport layer ensures reliable and efficient data delivery.

Basic concepts of computer networking include network topology, network protocols, addressing and naming, and network services. Network topology refers to the physical or logical layout of the network, such as bus, ring, star, or mesh. Network protocols define the rules and conventions for communication between devices on the network. Addressing and naming refer to how devices such as IP addresses or domain names are identified on the network. Network services provide specific functions or applications like email, web browsing, or file sharing.

Understanding the basics of computer networking is important for anyone working in computer science and engineering, as networking is a fundamental component of modern computing. By learning about the basic concepts and principles of computer networking, students can gain the knowledge and skills necessary to design, implement, and maintain computer networks for a wide range of applications.

TYPES OF COMPUTER NETWORK

There are several types of computer networks, including:

Local Area Network (LAN): A LAN is a network that covers a small geographic area, typically a single building or campus. LANs are used to connect devices such as computers, printers, and servers.

Wide Area Network (WAN): A WAN is a network that covers a large geographic area, such as a city, country, or even the world. WANs connect devices across long distances and are typically used by s with multiple locations.

Metropolitan Area Network (MAN): A MAN is a network that covers a larger geographic area than a LAN but is smaller than a WAN. A MAN is typically used to connect devices in a single city or metropolitan area.

Wireless Local Area Network (WLAN): A WLAN is a type of LAN that uses wireless communication to connect devices instead of physical cables. WLANs are commonly used in public spaces such as airports, coffee shops, and hotels.

Personal Area Network (PAN): A PAN is a network that connects devices near an individual, such as a smartphone, tablet, or laptop. Bluetooth is a common technology used for PANs.

Campus Area Network (CAN): A CAN is a network that covers a college or university campus, connecting buildings, departments, and dormitories.

Storage Area Network (SAN): A SAN is a specialised network designed to provide access to data storage. SANs are typically used by s that require high-speed access to large amounts of data, such as video production companies.

Virtual Private Network (VPN): A VPN is a network that provides a secure connection over a public network, such as the Internet. VPNs are commonly used to allow remote workers to access company resources securely.

Cloud Network: A cloud network is a type of network that utilizes cloud computing technologies to provide access to resources and services over the Internet.

Peer-to-Peer Network (P2P): A P2P network is a decentralized network where devices communicate directly without needing a central server. P2P networks are commonly used for file sharing and communication applications.

NETWORK DEVICES

In a computer network, different types of network devices are used to facilitate communication between devices and enable the sharing of resources. The most common network devices include routers, switches, hubs, and modems.

Routers: A router is a network device that connects multiple networks and manages the flow of data between them. It receives data packets from one network, examines the destination address, and forwards them to the appropriate network. Routers use protocols such as IP to determine the best path for the data to reach its destination. They can also be used to provide security by blocking unwanted traffic.

Switches: A switch is a network device that connects devices within a network and facilitates communication between them. It receives data packets from a device and forwards them only to the destination device. Switches use MAC addresses to identify devices and maintain a table of MAC addresses to enable efficient data transfer. They can also be used to manage network traffic and improve network performance.

Hubs: A hub is a network device connecting multiple devices within a network and allowing them to communicate. It receives data packets from a device and broadcasts them to all other devices connected to the hub. This can result in network congestion and slow performance, especially in larger networks. Hubs are not commonly used in modern networks due to their limitations.

Modems: A modem is a network device that converts digital signals from a computer into analogue signals that can be transmitted over a telephone or cable line. It also converts analogue signals from the line into digital signals that a computer can process. Modems are commonly used to provide Internet access to devices.

To recap, routers connect and manage traffic between multiple networks, switches connect and facilitate communication between devices within a network, hubs connect and can cause congestion within a network, and modems convert digital signals to analogue signals for transmission over a telephone or cable line. Each of these network nodes is essential for the smooth operation of a computer network, as it facilitates communication and the distribution of resources among users.

NETWORK TOPOLOGIES

Network topology refers to the physical or logical arrangement of devices in a network. There are several types of network topologies, each with its own advantages and disadvantages.

Bus Topology: A bus topology consists of a single cable, called the backbone, to which all the devices in the network are connected. Data is transmitted along the backbone to all the devices on the network. This topology is easy to install and inexpensive, but it can be slow and susceptible to data collisions, which can cause network congestion.

Ring Topology: A ring topology consists of a closed cable loop with devices connected directly to the cable. Data is transmitted around the ring in one direction, and each device on the network receives the data in turn. This topology is efficient and has fewer collisions than a bus topology, but it can be expensive to install and difficult to reconfigure.

Star Topology: A star topology consists of a central hub or switches to which all the devices on the network are connected. Data is transmitted from the source device to the hub or switch, which then sends the data to the destination device. This topology is easy to install and performs better than a bus or ring topology, but it is more expensive and can be vulnerable to a single point of failure.

Mesh Topology: A mesh topology consists of multiple connections between devices, forming a web-like network. Data is transmitted along multiple paths to reach its destination, providing redundancy and fault tolerance. This topology is highly reliable and can provide high-speed connections, but it can be expensive to install and difficult to manage.

Advantages and disadvantages:

Bus topology: Advantages: Easy to install, inexpensive. Disadvantages: Slow, susceptible to data collisions.

Ring topology: Advantages: Efficient, fewer collisions. Disadvantages: Expensive to install, difficult to reconfigure.

Star topology: Advantages: Easy to install, better performance. Disadvantages: More expensive, vulnerable to a single point of failure.

Mesh topology: Advantages: Highly reliable, provide redundancy and fault tolerance and can provide high-speed connections. Disadvantages: Expensive to install, difficult to manage.

Examples of where they are used:

Bus topology: Small local area networks (LANs) with few devices.

Ring topology: Local area networks (LANs) in which devices are located close together, such as in a school or office.

Star topology: Large LANs or wide area networks (WANs) with many devices.

Mesh topology: Large WANs or networks with critical applications that require high reliability and redundancy, such as financial institutions or hospitals.

NETWORK ARCHITECTURE AND PROTOCOLS

Network architecture and protocols refer to the design and of a computer network's physical and logical components and the rules and conventions governing communication between devices on the network.

Network architecture involves several key elements, including the physical topology, network devices, network services, and network protocols. The physical topology refers to the physical layout of the network, such as bus, ring, star, or mesh. Network devices are the hardware components that make up the network, such as switches, routers, and servers. Network services provide specific functions or applications like email, web browsing, or file sharing. Network protocols are the rules and conventions for communication between devices on the network, such as the Transmission Control Protocol/Internet Protocol (TCP/IP).

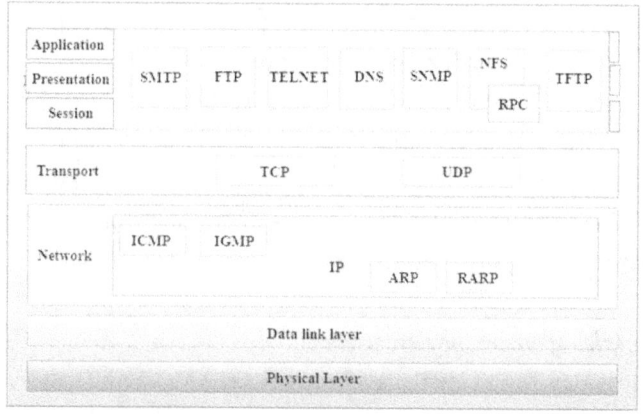

Figure 11 - Functions of TCP/IP layers

The TCP/IP protocol suite is the world's most widely used network protocol and is the Internet's foundation. It consists of several protocols, including the Internet Protocol (IP), responsible for addressing and routing data packets across the network, and the Transmission Control Protocol (TCP), responsible for ensuring reliable data delivery.

Other common network protocols include the User Datagram Protocol (UDP) for fast, low-latency communication and the Simple Mail Transfer Protocol (SMTP) for sending and receiving email messages.

Understanding network architecture and protocols is important for designing, implementing, and maintaining computer networks. By learning about the different components of network architecture and the rules and conventions of network protocols, students can gain the knowledge and skills necessary to create and manage efficient and reliable computer networks.

DIFFERENT TYPES OF NETWORK PROTOCOLS

HTTP (Hypertext Transfer Protocol): A protocol used for transferring hypertext (text, images, videos, etc.) across the internet. Web browsers use it to request and receive web pages from web servers.

FTP (File Transfer Protocol): A protocol used for transferring files over a network. It is often used to upload and download files from a web server.

SMTP (Simple Mail Transfer Protocol): A protocol used for sending email messages between email servers. It is responsible for sending messages from the sender's email server to the recipient's email server.

POP (Post Office Protocol): A protocol for retrieving email messages from a mail server. Email clients use it to download messages from the mail server to the client's device.

Each protocol has a specific function and works differently in a network. HTTP, for example, uses the request-response model, where a client sends a request to a server, and the server responds with the requested resource. On the other hand, FTP uses a client-server model, where the client connects to the FTP server and requests to upload or download files. SMTP uses a store-and-forward model, where the email server stores the message and forwards it to the recipient's email server.

Network protocols are essential for communication between devices on a network. They define the rules and conventions for data transfer and help ensure efficient and reliable communication.

NETWORK ADMINISTRATION

Network administration involves managing and maintaining computer networks, ensuring that they run smoothly, securely, and efficiently. Some of the key responsibilities of a network administrator include:

Network monitoring: Network administrators monitor network performance and identify potential issues before they affect users. This includes monitoring network traffic, identifying bottlenecks, and troubleshooting network issues.

Security management: Network administrators are responsible for securing the network against unauthorized access, viruses, and other security threats. They must implement security policies, monitor security logs, and configure firewalls and other security systems.

User management: Network administrators are responsible for creating and managing user accounts, assigning permissions, and providing technical support to users.

To become a network administrator, one should have a good understanding of computer networks and operating systems and knowledge of network protocols, security systems, and network administration tools. A degree in computer science or a related field is typically required, along with industry certifications such as Cisco Certified Network Associate (CCNA) or CompTIA Network+.

Some standard network administration tools include:

Network monitoring tools: These tools monitor network traffic and provide real-time information on network performance, including bandwidth utilisation, packet loss, and latency. Examples include Nagios, PRTG, and SolarWinds.

Security management tools: These tools help network administrators manage and secure the network against threats such as viruses, malware, and unauthorised access. Examples include firewalls, antivirus software, and intrusion detection systems.

User management tools: These tools help network administrators manage user accounts, permissions, and access. Examples include Microsoft Active Directory, LDAP, and RADIUS.

Network administration involves managing and maintaining computer networks to ensure they run efficiently and securely. Network administrators monitor network performance, security, and user accounts. To become a network administrator, one should have a good understanding of computer networks and operating systems and knowledge of network protocols, security systems, and network administration tools.

NETWORK STANDARDS

Ethernet, Wi-Fi, and Bluetooth are all examples of network standards that enable communication between devices in a network.

Ethernet is a wired networking technology that uses cables to transmit data between devices. It operates on the OSI model's physical and data link layers and supports various data transfer rates. Ethernet has evolved, with newer standards such as Gigabit Ethernet and 10 Gigabit Ethernet providing faster data transfer rates.

Wi-Fi is a wireless networking technology that uses radio waves to transmit data between devices. Wi-Fi allows devices to connect to a network without the need for physical cables, making it a popular choice for home and office networks. It operates on the OSI model's physical and data link layers and supports various wireless standards, including 802.11a, 802.11b, 802.11g, 802.11n, and 802.11ac.

Bluetooth is a wireless technology that enables short-range communication between devices, typically within 10 meters. It operates on the OSI model's physical and data link layers and is used for low-bandwidth applications such as wireless headphones, speakers, and keyboards.

All three standards are governed by various s, such as the Institute of Electrical and Electronics Engineers (IEEE), and they have their own unique characteristics and advantages. For example, Ethernet is faster and more reliable than Wi-Fi, while Wi-Fi offers more flexibility and convenience. Bluetooth is ideal for short-range communication between devices and is often used in consumer electronics products.

Understanding network standards is important for network administrators, as it allows them to choose the appropriate technology for their network infrastructure and devices. It also helps ensure that devices from different manufacturers can communicate with each other, as they all adhere to the same standards.

NETWORK CERTIFICATION

Network certifications are essential in the IT industry as they provide a way for professionals to demonstrate their knowledge and expertise in networking. Here are some key points to consider:

CCNA (Cisco Certified Network Associate), Network+, and CCNP (Cisco Certified Network Professional) are all examples of popular network certifications.

Network certifications demonstrate to employers that you have the knowledge and skills to design, install, configure, and troubleshoot complex computer networks.

Some benefits of getting certified include increased job opportunities, higher salaries, and the ability to work with more complex networking technologies.

To become certified, candidates typically need to pass an exam covering a range of networking topics, such as network fundamentals, routing and switching, and network security.

In addition to technical skills, candidates may need good problem-solving and communication skills to pass the exams and succeed in a network administration role.

Some examples of network administration tools that can help professionals prepare for certification exams include GNS3, Wireshark, and Cisco Packet Tracer.

Network certifications can be an important stepping stone for professionals looking to advance their careers in the IT industry. They demonstrate a commitment to ongoing learning and development and can provide a solid foundation for a successful career in network administration.

NETWORK SECURITY AND CRYPTOGRAPHY

Network security and cryptography refer to the techniques and practices used to protect computer networks and the data transmitted over them from unauthorised access, theft, or damage.

Network security involves several key concepts, including authentication, authorisation, and encryption. Authentication is the process of verifying the identity of a user or device trying to access the network. Authorisation is the process of granting or denying access to specific resources or services based on a user's or device's authentication credentials. Encryption is converting plain text data into a coded format, which those with the appropriate decryption key can only read.

Cryptography is a set of mathematical techniques used to secure data and communications. Cryptography involves several concepts, including symmetric encryption, asymmetric encryption, and digital signatures. Symmetric encryption uses a single key for both encryption and decryption, while asymmetric encryption uses separate public and private keys for encryption and decryption. Digital signatures are used to authenticate the identity of the sender of a message.

Other common techniques used for network security include firewalls, intrusion detection and prevention systems, virtual private networks (VPNs), and security protocols such as Secure Sockets Layer (SSL) and Transport Layer Security (TLS).

Understanding network security and cryptography is important for designing and implementing secure computer networks.

ENCRYPTION AND CRYPTOGRAPHY – USE CASES

Encryption and cryptography are used in various applications and industries to protect sensitive data and communications. Here are a few examples:

Secure communication: Encryption is commonly used to secure communications over the Internet, such as email, messaging, and voice calls. Encryption transforms the data into an unreadable format, which can only be decrypted by authorised users who possess the appropriate decryption key.

E-commerce: Online shopping and e-commerce sites use encryption to protect sensitive data, such as credit card numbers and personal information, during online transactions. The encryption ensures that the data is transmitted securely and cannot be intercepted or stolen by unauthorised parties.

Banking: Banks and financial institutions use cryptography to secure their online banking systems and transactions. Encryption protects customer data and prevents unauthorised access to financial accounts.

Healthcare: The healthcare industry uses encryption to protect patient data, including medical records, personal information, and financial data. Encryption is also used to secure communications between healthcare providers and patients, ensuring that sensitive information is kept confidential.

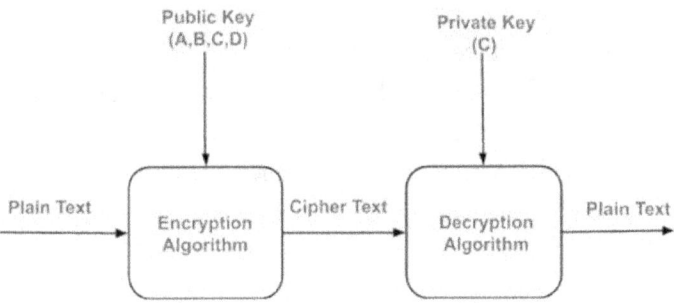

Figure 12 - Cryptography and Security in Banking

Government: Governments use encryption and cryptography to secure sensitive data and communications. Military and intelligence agencies use encryption to protect classified information, while law enforcement agencies use encryption to protect discreet investigations.

Encryption and cryptography are critical in securing sensitive data and communications in various industries and applications. By using encryption and cryptography, s can protect their data from unauthorised access and theft and ensure the privacy and confidentiality of their communications.

EXERCISES

1. What is a network protocol, and why is it important for computer networking?
2. Explain the concept of a physical topology in a computer network, and give an example of each of the following: bus, ring, star, and mesh.
3. What are the different layers in the TCP/IP protocol suite, and what is the function of each layer?

4. What is encryption, and how is it used to protect data in a computer network? Provide an example of an encryption technique.
5. Describe the process of authentication and authorization in a computer network.
6. Explain the difference between symmetric and asymmetric encryption, and give an example of each.
7. What is a firewall, and how does it protect a computer network from security threats?
8. Describe the purpose of a virtual private network (VPN), and how it is used to secure remote connections to a network.
9. What is a denial-of-service (DoS) attack, and how can it be prevented in a computer network?
10. Explain the importance of network security in the healthcare industry, and describe how encryption is used to protect sensitive patient data.

KEY TAKEAWAYS

- Computer networking is connecting computers and other devices to share resources and communicate.
- Basic concepts of computer networking include network topology, network protocols, addressing and naming, and network services.
- Network architecture and protocols refer to the design and of a computer network's physical and logical components and the rules and conventions governing communication between devices on the network.
- Network security and cryptography refer to the techniques and practices used to protect computer networks and the data transmitted over them from unauthorised access, theft, or damage.
- Different types of network devices include routers, switches, hubs, and modems, and each device plays a specific role in a network.

- Different network topologies include bus, ring, star, and mesh, each with advantages and disadvantages.
- Different network protocols such as HTTP, FTP, SMTP, and POP have specific functions and enable communication and data transfer between devices on a network.
- Network administration is responsible for monitoring, securing, and managing a network and requires specific skills and tools to perform these tasks effectively.
- Network standards such as Ethernet, Wi-Fi, and Bluetooth are essential in enabling communication and data transfer between devices on a network.
- Network certifications such as CCNA, Network+, and CCNP are valuable in demonstrating expertise in network administration and providing career opportunities in the field.

EXERCISE ANSWERS

1. A network protocol is a set of rules governing how data is transmitted over a network. It is important for computer networking because it ensures that devices can communicate with each other in a standardised way, enabling reliable and efficient data transfer.

2. Physical topology refers to the physical layout of a computer network. Examples of physical topologies include bus (devices are connected to a common backbone), ring (devices are connected in a closed loop), star (devices are connected to a central hub), and mesh (devices are connected to each other in a network of interconnections).

3. The TCP/IP protocol suite has four layers: the network access layer, the internet layer, the transport layer, and the application layer. The function of each layer is to provide a specific set of services that support the overall functioning of the network.

4. Encryption is the process of converting plaintext data into a coded format, which can only be read by authorised users who

possess the appropriate decryption key. An example of an encryption technique is Advanced Encryption Standard (AES), which is commonly used in wireless networks and online communications.

5. Authentication is the process of verifying the identity of a user or device trying to access a network, while authorisation is the process of granting or denying access to specific resources or services based on a user's or device's authentication credentials.

6. Symmetric encryption uses a single key for both encryption and decryption, while asymmetric encryption uses separate public and private keys for encryption and decryption. An example of symmetric encryption is Data Encryption Standard (DES), while an example of asymmetric encryption is RSA.

7. A firewall is a network security device that monitors and filters incoming and outgoing network traffic based on an organisation's previously established security policies. It protects a computer network from security threats by blocking unauthorised access to the network.

8. A virtual private network (VPN) is a network technology that enables secure remote connections to a private network over the public internet. It is used to provide remote users with secure access to a network's resources.

9. A denial-of-service (DoS) attack aims to disrupt a network's normal functioning by overwhelming it with traffic. It can be prevented in a computer network by implementing measures such as firewalls and intrusion detection and prevention systems.

10. Network security is crucial in the healthcare industry to protect sensitive patient data, including medical records, personal information, and financial data. Encryption is used to protect this data by converting it into a coded format, which can only be read by authorised users who possess the appropriate decryption key.

CLOUD COMPUTING

Cloud computing refers to delivering computing services over the Internet, such as servers, storage, databases, software, and networking. Instead of maintaining their computing infrastructure, s can access these services on demand from a cloud service provider, allowing them to scale up or down as needed.

There are three main types of cloud computing services: Software as a Service (SaaS), Platform as a Service (PaaS), and Infrastructure as a Service (IaaS).

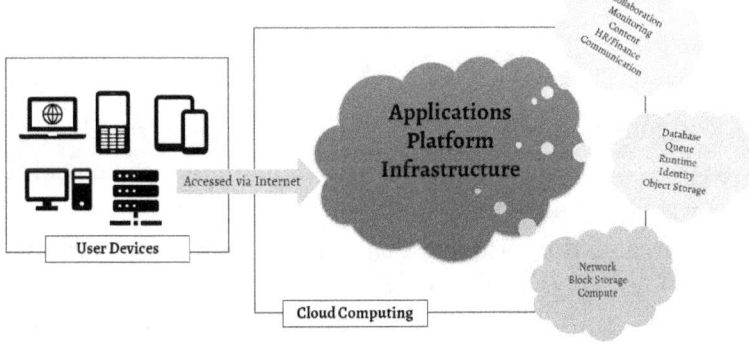

Figure 13 - Accessing cloud resources

SaaS: SaaS is a software delivery model where users access web applications. The software is hosted by a third-party provider and accessed through a web browser or mobile app. Examples of SaaS applications include Google Workspace, Salesforce, and Dropbox.

PaaS: PaaS provides a platform for developers to build, test, and deploy applications. PaaS providers offer a pre-configured environment that includes an operating system, database, and programming language, allowing developers to focus on building their applications. Examples of PaaS providers include Microsoft Azure, Amazon Web Services (AWS), and Google Cloud Platform.

IaaS: IaaS provides computing resources, such as virtual machines, storage, and networking, over the Internet. s can use these resources to run their applications or build their platforms. Examples of IaaS providers include AWS, Microsoft Azure, and Google Cloud Platform.

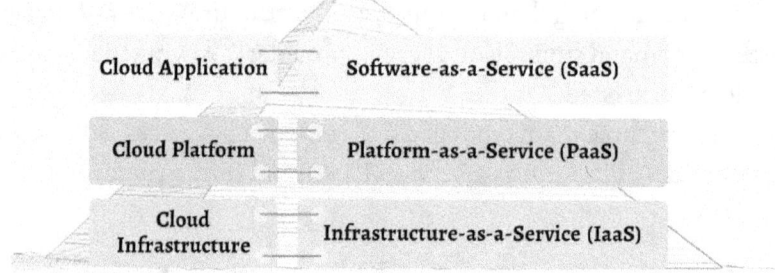

Figure 14 - Cloud computing services

Cloud computing offers several benefits, including scalability, cost-effectiveness, and flexibility. With cloud computing, s can quickly scale up or down as needed without investing in expensive hardware or software. Cloud computing also offers pay-as-you-go pricing, which allows s to only pay for the resources they use.

Cloud computing allows s to access their data and applications from anywhere, making collaborating and working remotely easier.

CLOUD DEPLOYMENT MODELS

Cloud deployment models refer to how cloud computing services are delivered and managed. There are four main cloud deployment models:

Public cloud: A public cloud is a cloud service provided by a third-party provider over the Internet. Public cloud providers offer computing resources that are shared among multiple customers, such as virtual machines, storage, and networking. Examples of public cloud providers include Amazon Web Services (AWS), Microsoft Azure, and Google Cloud Platform.

Private cloud: A private cloud is a cloud service owned and operated by a single. Large s typically use private clouds that require greater control and security over their computing infrastructure. Private clouds can be hosted on-premises or provided by a third-party provider.

Hybrid cloud: A hybrid cloud combines public and private clouds. s can run some applications and data in a public cloud in a hybrid cloud while keeping other applications and data in a private cloud. This allows s to take advantage of the scalability and cost-effectiveness of the public cloud while maintaining greater control over their data.

Multi-cloud: A multi-cloud environment uses multiple cloud services from different providers. This can include public and private clouds, as well as different types of cloud services, such as software as a Service (SaaS), Platform as a Service (PaaS), and Infrastructure as a Service (IaaS). Multi-cloud environments reduce the risk of vendor lock-in and improve resilience and redundancy.

BENEFITS AND DRAWBACKS OF CLOUD COMPUTING

Cloud computing offers several benefits, such as:

Scalability: Cloud computing allows s to quickly scale up or down as needed without investing in expensive hardware or software. This makes it easier for s to manage their computing resources and adjust to changing business needs.

Cost-effectiveness: With cloud computing, s can take advantage of pay-as-you-go pricing, allowing them to only pay for their resources. This can significantly reduce IT costs and help s optimise their budgets.

Flexibility: Cloud computing allows s to access their data and applications from anywhere, making collaborating and working remotely easier. Cloud computing also offers a wide range of services and features, allowing s to choose the best services.

However, there are also potential drawbacks to cloud computing, such as:

Security and privacy concerns: With cloud computing, s entrust their data to third-party providers. This raises concerns about data security and privacy, particularly in industries that handle sensitive data, such as healthcare and finance.

Reliance on internet connectivity: Cloud computing relies on reliable internet connectivity. If internet connectivity is slow or unreliable, it can affect the performance and accessibility of cloud services.

Vendor lock-in: Switching between cloud providers can be difficult and costly, making it challenging for s to move their computing infrastructure to a different provider.

Regulatory compliance: s may need to comply with specific regulations, such as data privacy laws, that can affect how they store and manage their data in the cloud.

CLOUD COMPUTING IN DAILY LIFE

Cloud computing is used in a variety of ways in daily life. Here are some examples:

Online file storage: Cloud storage services like Google Drive, Dropbox, and OneDrive allow users to store and access files and documents from anywhere with an internet connection. This makes it easy to collaborate on projects with colleagues and access important files while on the go.

Email and communication: Many email services, such as Gmail and Outlook, are cloud-based. This means that users can access their emails and other communication tools from any device with an internet connection.

Social media: Social media platforms like Facebook, Instagram, and Twitter use cloud computing to store user data and content. This allows users to access their profiles and content from any device with an internet connection.

Entertainment: Streaming services like Netflix, Spotify, and YouTube use cloud computing to store and deliver content to users. This allows users to access movies, TV shows, music, and other content from anywhere with an internet connection.

Online shopping: Many e-commerce sites like Amazon, eBay, and Alibaba use cloud computing to manage their online stores and process transactions. This allows users to shop from anywhere with an internet connection and have their purchases delivered to their doorstep.

CLOUD COMPUTING AND THE DIGITAL DIVIDE

The digital divide refers to the unequal distribution of access to and use of information and communication technologies (ICTs), such as computers, the internet, and mobile devices, among different social groups. It is a global issue affecting individuals, communities, and countries in developed and developing regions.

Several factors contribute to the digital divide, including socioeconomic status, geography, age, gender, education, and language. Those with access to ICTs and digital literacy skills can take advantage of the benefits of technology, such as educational and employment opportunities. In contrast, those who lack access may be left behind.

The digital divide has several implications for society. For example, it can lead to inequalities in education, health care, and economic opportunities. Those who are digitally excluded may not have access to online resources and services critical for their personal and professional growth. This can perpetuate social and economic disparities as the disadvantaged are further marginalised.

Cloud computing can be both a solution and a challenge to the digital divide. On the one hand, cloud computing can provide access to computing resources and services to those who would not otherwise have access to them. For example, cloud-based education platforms can enable students in remote or underprivileged areas to access educational resources and opportunities. On the other hand, the digital divide can also affect access to cloud services, as those who lack access to the internet or digital devices may not be able to take advantage of these services.

It is essential to address the digital divide to ensure that everyone has equal access to the benefits of technology. Governments, private s, and civil society can work together to promote digital inclusion by providing access to affordable internet, digital literacy training programs, and support for underrepresented communities to participate in the digital economy.

CLOUD COMPUTING USE CASES

Cloud computing has significantly impacted industries such as healthcare, education, and finance by enabling new innovations and advancements that were previously impossible.

In healthcare, cloud computing has enabled healthcare providers to store and manage patient data more efficiently and securely. With cloud computing, healthcare providers can access patient records from anywhere, collaborate with other healthcare providers in real time, and use advanced analytics to identify patterns and trends in patient data. Cloud computing has also enabled the development of telemedicine, which allows patients to receive medical care remotely through video consultations, reducing the need for in-person appointments and increasing access to healthcare for patients in remote areas.

In education, cloud computing has transformed the way students learn and access educational resources. With cloud-based learning management systems (LMS), students can access course materials, participate in online discussions, and collaborate with classmates from anywhere. Cloud computing has also enabled the development of massive open online courses (MOOCs), which provide free or low-cost access to high-quality educational content from leading universities and institutions worldwide.

In finance, cloud computing has enabled financial institutions to process and analyse large amounts of data more efficiently and accurately. With cloud computing, financial institutions can use advanced analytics to identify patterns and trends in market data, manage risk more effectively, and develop new financial products and services. Cloud computing has also enabled the development of fintech startups, leveraging cloud-based technologies to provide innovative financial products and services to consumers and businesses.

Cloud computing has had a transformative impact on industries such as healthcare, education, and finance, enabling innovations and advancements that were previously not possible.

VIRTUALISATION

Virtualisation refers to creating a virtual version of something, such as a server, operating system, storage device, or network. This allows multiple virtual instances to run on a single physical machine, allowing for better resource utilisation and increased efficiency.

Examples of virtualization include:

Server virtualisation: In server virtualisation, a physical server is divided into multiple virtual servers, each running its own operating system and applications. This allows for better utilisation of server resources and increased flexibility in managing workloads.

Operating system virtualisation: In operating system virtualisation, a single physical machine can run multiple virtual instances of an operating system, creating isolated environments for testing or running applications.

Storage virtualisation: In storage virtualisation, multiple physical storage devices are combined into a single virtual storage pool, allowing for more efficient use of storage resources and easier data management.

Network virtualization: In network virtualisation, a physical network is divided into multiple virtual networks, allowing for better isolation and security of network traffic.

Virtualisation allows for more efficient use of computing resources and greater flexibility in managing workloads, making it a key technology in modern computing.

SERVERLESS COMPUTING

Serverless computing is a cloud computing model where the cloud provider manages the infrastructure and automatically allocates resources as needed for running applications. In this model, the cloud provider abstracts away the underlying hardware and infrastructure, so developers can focus on writing code for their applications without worrying about managing servers or infrastructure.

In serverless computing, applications are broken down into small, self-contained functions that can be executed independently. Specific events, such as user requests or changes to a data source, trigger these functions. When activated, the cloud provider automatically allocates the necessary resources to run the function and deallocates them when it is complete.

Examples of serverless computing include AWS Lambda, Google Cloud Functions, and Azure Functions. For example, AWS Lambda allows developers to write code in multiple programming languages and automatically scales the execution of the code based on demand. This allows developers to focus on writing code that responds to specific events and reduces the need for managing infrastructure.

EXERCISES

1. What is the difference between Software as a Service (SaaS) and Platform as a Service (PaaS)? Give an example of each and explain their advantages and disadvantages.
2. What are the benefits and drawbacks of using a public and private cloud? Give an example of an industry that might prefer one over the other.
3. What is the digital divide, and how does it relate to cloud computing? Discuss the potential consequences of a digital divide in terms of access to cloud services.
4. Discuss the importance of data privacy and security in cloud computing. What are some best practices for protecting sensitive data in the cloud?
5. How has cloud computing impacted the way businesses operate? Give examples of businesses that have leveraged cloud computing to improve efficiency and productivity.

KEY TAKEAWAYS

- Cloud computing refers to delivering computing services over the Internet, such as servers, storage, databases, software, and networking.
- The three main types of cloud computing services are Software as a Service (SaaS), Platform as a Service (PaaS), and Infrastructure as a Service (IaaS).
- Cloud deployment models include public, private, hybrid, and multi-cloud.

- Cloud computing offers several benefits, including scalability, cost-effectiveness, and flexibility, but there are also potential drawbacks, such as security and privacy concerns and reliance on internet connectivity.
- Cloud computing has significantly impacted various industries, including healthcare, education, and finance, enabling new innovations and advancements.
- Ethical and societal considerations around cloud computing include data privacy, security, and the digital divide.
- Cloud computing requires certain skills, such as knowledge of cloud architecture, security, and networking. There are various cloud certifications available for those interested in pursuing a career in cloud computing.

EXERCISE ANSWERS

1. What are the three main types of cloud computing services?
    i. Software as a Service (SaaS)
    ii. Platform as a Service (PaaS)
    iii. Infrastructure as a Service (IaaS)
2. What are the four main cloud deployment models?
    i. Public cloud
    ii. Private cloud
    iii. Hybrid cloud
    iv. Multi-cloud
3. What are some potential benefits of cloud computing?
    i. Scalability
    ii. Cost-effectiveness
    iii. Flexibility
4. What are some potential drawbacks of cloud computing?
    i. Security and privacy concerns
    ii. Reliance on internet connectivity
    iii. Vendor lock-in

          iv. Regulatory compliance

5. What are some ethical and societal considerations around cloud computing?

          i. Data privacy

          ii. Security

          iii. Digital divide

EDGE COMPUTING

Edge computing is a model for delivering computing resources that brings computation and data storage closer to the devices that use them. Some of the basic concepts and topics related to edge computing include:

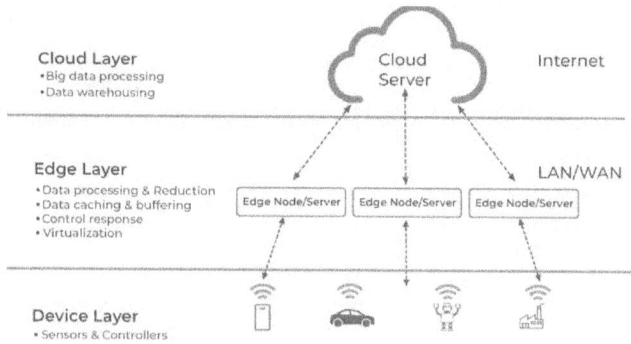

Figure 15 - Edge computing architecture

BASICS OF EDGE COMPUTING

Edge computing is a form of distributed computing that involves processing data and performing analytics at or near the edge of a network rather than in a centralised location like a data centre or the cloud.

Edge computing is designed to overcome some of the limitations of cloud computing, such as latency, bandwidth limitations, and the need for real-time processing. By processing data at the network's edge, s can reduce the amount of data that needs to be sent to the cloud, improving network performance and reducing costs.

Edge computing is used in various applications, such as autonomous vehicles, industrial automation, and healthcare. For example, edge computing can be used in autonomous vehicles to process data from sensors and cameras in real time, allowing the vehicle to make decisions quickly and safely. In healthcare, edge computing can monitor patients and provide real-time feedback on their health status.

One of the benefits of edge computing is that it enables s to make more informed decisions in real time. s can quickly analyse and act on data by processing data at the network's edge rather than waiting for data to be processed to the cloud. Edge computing also provides greater flexibility, allowing s to process data where it makes the most sense for their business.

However, edge computing has potential drawbacks, such as the need for greater device management and security and specialised skills to manage the distributed computing environment. By understanding the benefits and drawbacks of edge computing, s can determine whether it is the right approach for their needs.

EDGE COMPUTING ARCHITECTURE

Edge computing architecture involves distributing computing resources from the cloud to the network's edge to improve data processing and reduce latency. There are several architectures used in edge computing, including:

Cloud-based edge computing: In this architecture, the cloud provider deploys computing resources near the network's edge to reduce latency and improve response times. The edge devices communicate with cloud-based resources to access data and services.

Fog computing: This architecture distributes computing resources from the cloud to the network's edge, creating a distributed computing environment that can perform data processing, storage, and analytics. Fog computing nodes are typically located in local data centres, network hubs, or on-premises infrastructure.

Mobile edge computing: In this architecture, some of the computing tasks are offloaded to mobile devices, such as smartphones or tablets, to reduce latency and improve performance. The mobile devices act as edge nodes, performing data processing and analytics while communicating with the cloud-based resources.

Hybrid edge computing: This architecture combines different edge computing architectures to create a more flexible and scalable environment. It can involve a combination of cloud-based edge computing, fog computing, and mobile edge computing to meet the application's specific needs.

Edge computing architecture offers several benefits: faster data processing and response times, reduced network congestion and bandwidth usage improved security and privacy, and increased scalability and flexibility. By distributing computing resources closer to the network's edge, s can optimise their computing infrastructure and better meet the demands of modern, data-intensive applications.

ADVANTAGES OVER TRADITIONAL CLOUD COMPUTING

Edge computing has several advantages over traditional cloud computing, such as:

Reduced latency: Edge computing enables faster processing and response times by bringing computing resources closer to where data is being generated. This reduces the latency associated with sending data to the cloud for processing.

Increased privacy and security: Edge computing can provide greater privacy and security, as data is processed and stored locally rather than being sent to the cloud. This can be particularly important for industries that handle sensitive data, such as healthcare and finance.

Bandwidth optimisation: Edge computing can help reduce network congestion and optimise bandwidth usage by processing data locally and sending only the most important data to the cloud for further processing and storage.

Real-time processing: Edge computing enables real-time processing and decision-making, which can be critical in applications such as autonomous vehicles, industrial automation, and healthcare.

Cost-effectiveness: Edge computing can be more cost-effective than cloud computing, as it can reduce the need for expensive cloud services and infrastructure.

Edge computing provides a more distributed computing environment that can better meet the demands of modern, data-intensive applications.

By combining edge and cloud computing benefits, s can optimise their computing infrastructure and better serve their customers.

HYBRID CLOUD AND EDGE COMPUTING

Hybrid cloud and edge computing are two computing paradigms that can be used together to create a powerful and flexible computing environment.

A hybrid cloud uses public and private infrastructures to host applications and data. By using a hybrid cloud, and can take advantage of the scalability and cost-effectiveness of the public cloud while maintaining greater control over their data by using a private cloud.

On the other hand, Edge computing refers to the processing and storage of data at or near the network's edge, close to the devices that generate and use the data. s can reduce latency, improve network performance, and reduce costs by processing data at the edge.

Combining hybrid cloud and edge computing allows s to create of a computing environment that is both flexible and powerful. In this architecture, the public cloud can host applications and data that require significant computing resources. In contrast, the private cloud can store and process sensitive data. Edge computing can process data generated by devices at the network's edge in real-time, allowing organisations to make faster and more informed decisions.

For example, a retailer could use a hybrid cloud to host their e-commerce website and store customer data in a private cloud. They could use edge computing to process data generated by sensors in their physical stores, such as foot traffic and product placements, to make real-time decisions about store layouts and marketing campaigns. By combining these technologies, the retailer could improve their overall customer experience and increase sales.

In essence, combining hybrid cloud and edge computing allows the creation of a computing environment that is both scalable and secure while also allowing for real-time processing of data at the edge of the network. This architecture is becoming increasingly popular as s seek to take advantage of the benefits of both cloud and edge computing.

EDGE COMPUTING AND THE INTERNET OF THINGS (IoT)

Edge computing and the Internet of Things (IoT) are closely related technologies often used together to support real-time data processing and analysis. IoT involves using sensors and connected devices to collect data from various sources. At the same time, edge computing requires processing and analyzing this data at or near the source of the data rather than transmitting it to a centralised cloud environment for processing.

Combining edge computing and IoT benefits applications that require low latency and real-time processing, such as industrial automation, autonomous vehicles, and healthcare. Processing data at the edge in these applications allows for faster decision-making and improved system performance.

Edge computing can also help reduce the amount of data that must be transmitted to the cloud for processing, which can help reduce network congestion and lower costs. By processing data at the edge, s can also improve data privacy and security by minimising the amount of sensitive data that needs to be transmitted over the network.

Combining edge computing and IoT is a powerful approach for enabling real-time data processing and analysis. It is becoming increasingly important as more devices become connected and more data is generated at the edge of networks.

USE CASES AND EXAMPLES

Autonomous vehicles: Edge computing processes data from sensors and cameras in real time, allowing the vehicle to make decisions quickly and safely.

Industrial automation: Edge computing monitors and controls industrial processes in real time, improving efficiency and reducing downtime.

Healthcare: Edge computing monitors patients and provides real-time feedback on their health status, enabling healthcare professionals to make more informed decisions.

Smart cities: Edge computing is used to collect and analyse data from sensors and cameras located throughout the city, allowing s to manage traffic better, reduce energy consumption, and improve public safety.

Retail: Edge computing is used to analyse data from in-store cameras and sensors, providing retailers with insights into customer behaviour and improving the shopping experience.

Energy: Edge computing monitors and controls energy systems in real-time, improving efficiency and reducing costs.

Agriculture: Edge computing monitors and optimises crop conditions, reducing waste and improving yields.

In general, edge computing is employed in many contexts where the need for low latency, fast processing, and secure data transmission cannot be overstated. Edge computing allows for novel uses in many fields since it places processing power near the source of data creation.

EDGE COMPUTING USE CASES IN THE ENTERTAINMENT

Edge computing has a range of use cases in the entertainment industry, particularly in areas such as video streaming, gaming, and virtual reality. Here are some examples:

Video streaming: Edge computing can reduce buffering and improve video quality in real time. By processing video data closer to the end-user, edge computing can reduce the latency of sending video data to the cloud for processing. This can improve the user experience and reduce the frustration associated with buffering and other video streaming issues.

Gaming: Edge computing can improve online games' performance by reducing latency and improving response times. By processing game data closer to the end-user, edge computing can provide a more seamless gaming experience, allowing players to enjoy fast and responsive gameplay.

Virtual reality (VR): Edge computing can improve VR applications' performance by reducing latency and improving response times. By processing VR data closer to the end-user, edge computing can provide a more immersive and responsive VR experience, allowing users to feel like they are truly part of the virtual world.

Live events: Edge computing can improve live events' performance, such as concerts and sporting events, by providing real-time data processing and analysis from cameras and other sensors. This can enable real-time video streaming and analysis, allowing viewers to feel like they are truly part of the live event.

Content delivery networks (CDNs): Edge computing can improve the performance of CDNs by distributing content delivery closer to end-users. By processing and caching content closer to end-users, edge computing can reduce the latency associated with content delivery and improve the overall user experience.

In general, edge computing can help the entertainment industry deliver better performance and a more seamless user experience across a range of applications and use cases.

EXERCISES

1. How does edge computing differ from cloud computing regarding data processing and storage?
2. Explain the concept of latency and how edge computing can help reduce it.
3. What are some of the challenges associated with managing edge computing infrastructure?
4. Describe some benefits and drawbacks of using edge computing in the healthcare industry.
5. Give an example of how edge computing can be used in industrial automation.
6. What are the key features of mobile edge computing, and how does it differ from other edge computing?
7. How can edge computing be used to improve the efficiency of energy systems?
8. Describe the architecture of a fog computing system, and give an example of how it can be used.
9. What are some ethical considerations around edge computing, particularly concerning data privacy and security?
10. Explain how edge computing can be used in the retail industry to improve customer experience and provide retailers with valuable insights.

KEY TAKEAWAYS

- Edge computing is a distributed computing model that involves processing data and performing analytics at or near the edge of a network rather than in a centralised location like a data centre or the cloud.
- Edge computing enables faster processing and response times, reduced latency, and real-time decision-making by bringing computing resources closer to where data is generated.
- Edge computing has several advantages over traditional cloud computing, including increased privacy and security, bandwidth optimisation, and cost-effectiveness.
- Edge computing requires specialised skills to manage the distributed computing environment and greater device management and security.
- Edge computing is commonly used in autonomous vehicles, industrial automation, healthcare, smart cities, retail, energy, and agriculture applications.
- Edge computing architectures can include fog computing, which involves distributing computing resources from the cloud to the edge of the network, and mobile edge computing, which involves offloading some computing tasks to mobile devices.
- Edge computing and IoT are closely related and are often used to provide real-time data processing and analysis in various applications.
- Edge computing is a key enabler of new innovations and advancements in various fields, such as entertainment, where it is used to enable real-time interactions and personalized experiences for users.
- Edge computing can help reduce network congestion, optimise bandwidth usage, and improve the performance and accessibility of cloud services.

- By understanding the benefits and drawbacks of edge computing, s can determine whether it is the right approach for their needs and optimise their computing infrastructure to serve their customers better.

EXERCISE ANSWERS

1. What is the main advantage of edge computing over cloud computing?
    a. Reduced latency
2. What is the main drawback of edge computing?
    a. The need for greater device management, security, and specialised skills to manage the distributed computing environment.
3. What is the difference between fog computing and mobile edge computing?
    a. Fog computing involves distributing computing resources from the cloud to the network's edge, while mobile edge computing consists of offloading some computing tasks to mobile devices.
4. In what industry is edge computing commonly used to monitor patients and provide real-time health status feedback?
    a. Healthcare
5. What is the benefit of using edge computing in autonomous vehicles?
    a. Edge computing processes data from sensors and cameras in real-time, allowing the vehicle to make decisions quickly and safely.
6. What is the benefit of using edge computing in industrial automation?
    a. Edge computing monitors and controls industrial processes in real-time, improving efficiency and reducing downtime.
7. How can edge computing help reduce network congestion?

      a.   By processing data locally and sending only the most important data to the cloud for further processing and storage.

8. What is the main benefit of combining edge and cloud computing?

      a.   Optimising computing infrastructure and better serving customers.

9. In what industry is edge computing commonly used for monitoring and optimising crop conditions?

      a.   Agriculture

10. What is the main benefit of using edge computing in retail?

      a.   Providing retailers with insights into customer behaviour and improving the shopping experience.

USABILITY AND INTERACTION

Usability and interaction refer to designing and evaluating computer interfaces that are easy to use and provide a positive user experience. The goal of usability and interaction design is to make technology more accessible and effective for a wider range of users.

Usability and interaction design involves several key principles, including:

User-centred design: User-centered design is a design philosophy that places the needs and preferences of the user at the centre of the design process. This involves gathering user feedback throughout the design process to ensure that the final product meets their needs.

Human-computer interaction: Human-computer interaction studies how people interact with computers and other digital devices. This includes research on user behaviour, cognitive processes, and physical ergonomics.

Usability testing and evaluation: Usability testing involves testing a product with real users to identify any problems or issues with the design. This feedback can be used to improve the design before it is released.

User experience design: User experience design is designing a product or service that provides a positive user experience. This involves considering the user's needs, expectations, and emotions throughout the design process.

Usability and interaction design is used in various applications, from mobile apps to web-based applications to industrial control systems. Good usability and interaction design can lead to higher user satisfaction, increased productivity, and reduced errors and user frustration.

Examples of usability and interaction design include intuitive user interfaces, voice-activated assistants, and touchscreen displays. By focusing on the user's needs and designing technology that is easy to use and understand, usability and interaction design are making technology more accessible and effective for people of all ages and abilities.

In summary, usability and interaction design are crucial in creating technology that is easy to use and provides a positive user experience. By considering the needs and preferences of the user, designing intuitive interfaces, and conducting usability testing and evaluation, designers can create products and services that are accessible and effective for people of all ages and abilities.

Usability and interaction design are important for improving user satisfaction and productivity and promoting inclusivity and diversity in technology. By designing for a wider range of users, including those with disabilities, language barriers, or other challenges, technology can become more inclusive and supportive of diverse communities.

While usability and interaction design principles may seem straightforward, achieving good usability and user experience can be complex and iterative, requiring careful research, prototyping, and testing. However, investing in usability and interaction design can lead to higher user adoption, customer loyalty, and business success in a competitive market.

As technology continues to evolve and become more ubiquitous in our daily lives, the importance of usability and interaction design will only grow. By staying up-to-date with the latest research, trends, and best practices in this field, designers and developers can create technology that truly serves the user's needs and improves their quality of life.

BASICS OF USER-CENTRED DESIGN

User-centred design (UCD) is a design philosophy that places the needs and preferences of the user at the centre of the design process. The goal of UCD is to create products and services that are effective, efficient, and satisfying for users.

UCD involves several key steps, including:

Research: UCD starts with understanding the needs and preferences of the users. This involves gathering feedback from users through surveys, interviews, and observations.

Design: Once the user needs have been identified, the next step is to design a product or service that meets those needs. This involves creating prototypes and conducting user testing to ensure that the design is effective and user-friendly.

Evaluation: Once the design is complete, the final step is to evaluate the product or service with real users. This can involve testing the product in a real-world environment or gathering user feedback through surveys or interviews.

UCD is used in various applications, from mobile apps to web-based applications to industrial control systems. Good UCD can increase user satisfaction and productivity and reduce errors and frustration.

Examples of UCD include intuitive user interfaces, user-friendly mobile apps, and easy-to-use industrial control systems. By focusing on the user's needs and designing technology that is easy to use and understand, UCD is making technology more accessible and effective for people of all ages and abilities.

HUMAN-COMPUTER INTERACTIONS (HCI)

HCI stands for Human-Computer Interaction. It is a field of study that focuses on designing and evaluating computer interfaces that are easy to use and provide a positive user experience. HCI is concerned with how people interact with computers and other digital devices and how the design of these devices can be improved to make them more accessible and effective for a broader range of users.

HCI is an interdisciplinary field combining computer science, psychology, design, and engineering elements. It involves the study of user behaviour, cognitive processes, and physical ergonomics, as well as the design of user interfaces, user testing, and evaluation.

HCI aims to create effective, efficient, and satisfying technology for users. This involves considering users' needs, preferences, and emotions throughout the design process and creating intuitive, easy-to-use, and aesthetically pleasing interfaces. Good HCI can increase user satisfaction and productivity and reduce errors and frustration.

PRINCIPLES OF HUMAN-COMPUTER INTERACTION

The principles of human-computer interaction (HCI) refer to designing and evaluating computer interfaces that are easy to use and provide a positive user experience. HCI aims to create effective, efficient, and satisfying technology for users.

Some of the key principles of HCI include:

Learnability: Interfaces with clear and concise user instructions should be easy to learn.

Flexibility: Interfaces should be flexible enough to accommodate a range of user needs and preferences.

Feedback: Interfaces should provide clear and immediate feedback to users, indicating what action has been taken and what the system is doing.

Error handling: Interfaces should be designed to prevent errors, but when errors do occur, they should be handled clearly and informally to users.

Consistency: Interfaces should be consistent in design and behaviour, with similar functions and commands behaving similarly across different applications and platforms.

Aesthetics: Interfaces should be visually appealing and designed with the user in mind, focusing on usability and accessibility.

By following these principles, designers can create interfaces that are easy to use and provide a positive user experience. This can lead to higher user satisfaction, increased productivity, and reduced errors and user frustration.

USABILITY TESTING AND EVALUATION

Usability testing and evaluation is a process used to assess the effectiveness and efficiency of computer interfaces and other digital products. The goal of usability testing is to identify any problems or issues with the design of a product and to make improvements to the design based on user feedback.

Usability testing typically involves several steps, including:

Identifying the user group: The first step in usability testing is to identify the target user group for the product. This may involve conducting surveys, interviews, or other research to gather information about user needs and preferences.

Creating test scenarios: Usability testers create test scenarios that simulate how users interact with the product in real-world situations. These scenarios test specific aspects of the product's design, such as navigation, functionality, and ease of use.

Conducting user testing: During user testing, testers observe users as they interact with the product and gather feedback on their experience. This feedback is used to identify any issues or problems with the product's design.

Analysing test results: The feedback gathered during user testing is analysed to identify patterns or trends in user behaviour. This information improves the product's design, such as changing the layout, adding or removing features, or improving the user interface.

Usability testing and evaluation are used in various applications, from mobile apps to web-based applications to industrial control systems.

USER EXPERIENCE (UX) DESIGN

User experience (UX) design is designing digital products and services that are easy to use and provide a positive user experience. UX design aims to create effective, efficient, and satisfying technology for users.

UX design involves several key steps, including:

User research: UX designers gather information about the product's users, including their needs, preferences, and behaviours.

Information architecture: UX designers organise the information and content of the product in a way that is easy to navigate and understand.

Interaction design: UX designers design the product's user interface and user interactions, focusing on creating a positive and intuitive user experience.

Visual design: UX designers create the visual design of the product, including the layout, colours, typography, and other visual elements.

User testing: UX designers conduct user testing to gather user feedback and identify issues or problems with the product's design.

Examples of good UX design can be seen in a wide range of digital products and services. For example:

- The user interface of Apple's iPhone is known for its intuitive and easy-to-use design. The interface is based on simple and recognisable icons with clear and concise text labels.
- The website of the travel company Airbnb is designed to be visually appealing and easy to navigate. The site uses large and high-quality images to showcase the properties, and the layout is organised to make it easy for users to search and book accommodations.
- The navigation and layout of the web-based productivity tool Trello are designed to be flexible and customisable. Users can easily add and move tasks, and the interface is designed to work for a wide range of use cases.

Accessibility: One of the key goals of HCI is to make digital devices and interfaces accessible to all users, including those with disabilities. Designers should consider factors such as screen reader compatibility, keyboard navigation, and colour contrast when creating interfaces.

Contextual Inquiry: Contextual inquiry is a research technique used in HCI to observe users in their natural environment and understand their needs and behaviours. This can provide valuable insights into how users interact with technology and inform the design process.

Persona creation: Persona creation is a technique used in UX design to create fictional characters that represent the product's target audience. Personas can help designers empathize with users and design products that meet their needs.

Iterative design: Iterative design is a design approach that involves creating and testing product prototypes multiple times throughout the design process. This can help identify and fix issues early on and create a more effective final product.

Emotional Design: Emotional design is a design approach that considers the emotional impact of a product on its users. Designers can create emotional connections with users through the use of colour, typography, and imagery, among other elements.

By following the principles of UX design and creating digital products that are easy to use and provide a positive user experience, designers can create technology that is accessible and effective for people of all ages and abilities.

EXERCISES

1. What is the purpose of usability and interaction design?
2. What are the principles of human-computer interaction (HCI)?
3. What are usability testing and evaluation?
4. What is user experience (UX) design?
5. What are some examples of good UX design?
6. What is the purpose of a prototype in usability and interaction design?
7. What is the importance of user feedback in usability and interaction design?
8. What is the role of cognitive psychology in HCI?
9. What is the importance of accessibility in usability and interaction design?
10. What is the goal of user-centred design?

KEY TAKEAWAYS

- Usability and interaction are essential for creating effective, efficient, and satisfying user technology.

- User-centred design is a key principle of usability and interaction, which involves placing the needs and preferences of the user at the centre of the design process.
- Human-computer interaction (HCI) is an interdisciplinary field combining computer science, psychology, design, and engineering elements.
- Usability testing and evaluation are used to assess the effectiveness and efficiency of computer interfaces and other digital products.
- User experience (UX) design involves gathering information about the product's users, organizing the information and content of the product, designing the product's user interface and interactions, creating the visual design, and conducting user testing.
- Consistency is an essential principle of usability and interaction, which involves designing interfaces that behave similarly across different applications and platforms.
- Feedback is another critical principle of usability and interaction, which involves providing clear and immediate feedback to users, indicating what action has been taken and what the system is doing.
- Error handling is also an essential principle of usability and interaction, which involves designing interfaces to prevent errors and handling errors clearly and informatively to users.
- Learnability is a principle of usability and interaction, which involves designing interfaces with clear and concise user instructions that are easy to learn.
- Flexibility is another important principle of usability and interaction, which involves designing interfaces that are flexible enough to accommodate a range of user needs and preferences.
- Aesthetics is also an essential principle of usability and interaction, which involves designing visually appealing interfaces with the user in mind, focusing on usability and accessibility.

- Usability and interaction design can lead to higher user satisfaction, increased productivity, and reduced errors and frustration.
- Usability and interaction design is used in various applications, from mobile apps to web-based applications to industrial control systems.
- Good usability and interaction design can make technology more accessible and effective for people of all ages and abilities.
- Usability testing and evaluation can help identify any problems or issues with the design of a product and make improvements to the design based on user feedback.
- User research is an essential step in UX design, which involves gathering information about the product's users, including their needs, preferences, and behaviours.
- Information architecture is another key step in UX design, which involves organising the information and content of the product in a way that is easy to navigate and understand.
- Interaction design is also an important step in UX design, which involves designing the product's user interface and user interactions, focusing on creating a positive and intuitive user experience.
- Visual design is another key step in UX design, which involves creating the product's visual design, including the layout, colours, typography, and other visual elements.
- User testing is an essential step in UX design, which involves conducting user testing to gather user feedback and identify issues or problems with the product's design.

EXERCISE ANSWERS

1. What is the purpose of usability and interaction design?
    - Usability and interaction design is focused on designing and evaluating computer interfaces that are easy to use and provide a positive user experience.

The goal is to make technology more accessible and effective for a wider range of users.

2. What are the principles of human-computer interaction (HCI)?

   - Some of the key principles of HCI include learnability, flexibility, feedback, error handling, consistency, and aesthetics. These principles are focused on creating interfaces that are easy to use and provide a positive user experience.

3. What are usability testing and evaluation?

   - Usability testing and evaluation is a process used to assess the effectiveness and efficiency of computer interfaces and other digital products. The goal of usability testing is to identify any problems or issues with the design of a product and to make improvements to the design based on user feedback.

4. What is user experience (UX) design?

   - User experience (UX) design is focused on designing digital products and services that are easy to use and provide a positive user experience. UX design involves several key steps, including user research, information architecture, interaction design, visual design, and user testing.

5. What are some examples of good UX design?

   - Examples of good UX design can be seen in a wide range of digital products and services, including the user interface of Apple's iPhone, the website of Airbnb, and the navigation and layout of the web-based productivity tool Trello.

6. What is the purpose of a prototype in usability and interaction design?

   - A prototype is a preliminary model or version of a product that is used to test and evaluate the design. A usability and interaction design prototype aims to identify any problems or issues with the design early in the development process, so that they can be addressed before the final product is released.

7. What is the importance of user feedback in usability and interaction design?

- User feedback is critical in usability and interaction design because it provides insights into how users interact with the product and identifies any problems or issues with the design. This feedback can be used to improve the design and create a product that better meets the needs of its users.

8. What is the role of cognitive psychology in HCI?

- Cognitive psychology concerns the mental processes that underlie human behaviour, including perception, attention, memory, and problem-solving. In HCI, cognitive psychology is used to understand how users interact with computer interfaces and how the design of these interfaces can be improved to make them more effective and efficient.

9. What is the importance of accessibility in usability and interaction design?

- Accessibility is critical in usability and interaction design because it ensures that the product is usable by people of all ages and abilities. By designing for accessibility, designers can create more inclusive products that provide a positive user experience for everyone.

10. What is the goal of user-centred design?

- The goal of user-centred design is to place the needs and preferences of the user at the centre of the design process. This involves gathering user feedback throughout the design process to ensure that the final product meets their needs and provides a positive user experience.

PROJECT WORK

Here is a list of projects associated with the subjects covered in this chapter. Students can work on any or all of these projects to validate their understanding of the topics covered in chapter 1:

BUILD A SIMPLE COMPUTER

Students can build a simple computer system by assembling hardware components such as a motherboard, CPU, RAM, and storage devices and then installing and configuring an operating system. This project will help them understand how hardware components work together and the basics of computer architecture.

DESIGN A NETWORK SECURITY PLAN

Students can design a network security plan for a small business or . This project will involve researching different network architectures and protocols, identifying potential security threats, and developing a plan to mitigate them using encryption, firewalls, and intrusion detection techniques.

DEVELOP A CLOUD APPLICATION

Students can develop a cloud-based application using a platform such as Amazon Web Services or Microsoft Azure. This project will help them understand the benefits and drawbacks of cloud computing and the different types of cloud services and give them hands-on experience working with cloud technology.

BUILD AN IOT DEVICE

Students can build a simple IoT device using a microcontroller like Arduino or Raspberry Pi. This project will help them understand the basics of edge computing and how IoT devices can collect and process data in real-time.

CONDUCT A USABILITY TEST

Students can conduct a usability test of a website or mobile application. This project will involve learning about user-centred design principles and usability testing and evaluation methods and applying these principles to improve the user experience of the website or application.

PROJECT HELP

Here are some tips and resources for each project:

Build a simple computer:
- Research and choose the hardware components carefully, making sure they are compatible with each other.
- Follow a step-by-step guide to assemble the computer, such as this one from PCPartPicker: https://pcpartpicker.com/guide/.
- Choose and install an operating system, such as Windows or Linux, and configure basic settings.
- Test the computer and troubleshoot any issues that arise.

Design a network security plan:
- Research different network architectures and security protocols, such as VPNs, firewalls, and intrusion detection systems.
- Identify potential security threats like malware, phishing, and DDoS attacks.

- Develop a plan to mitigate these threats, including implementing security protocols, training employees on safe computing practices, and regularly monitoring and updating security measures.
- Use tools like the NIST Cybersecurity Framework (https://www.nist.gov/cyberframework) to help guide your plan.

Develop a cloud application:

- Choose a cloud platform, such as Amazon Web Services or Microsoft Azure, and research its different services and capabilities.
- Decide on the type of application to develop, such as a web application or a mobile app, and choose the appropriate development tools and programming languages.
- Design and build the application using cloud services such as storage, databases, and serverless computing.
- Test the application and deploy it to the cloud platform.

Build an IoT device:

- Choose a microcontroller such as Arduino or Raspberry Pi, and research its capabilities and specifications.
- Decide on the type of IoT device to build, such as a smart thermostat or a weather station, and choose the appropriate sensors and components.
- Program the microcontroller to collect and process sensor data and send it to a cloud platform or mobile app for analysis and visualisation.
- Test the device and troubleshoot any issues that arise.

Conduct a usability test:

- Choose a website or mobile application to test, and recruit participants representing the target user group.

- Design and conduct a usability test, using methods such as surveys, interviews, and observation to gather participant feedback.
- Analyse the feedback and identify areas for improvement, such as navigation, layout, and content.
- Make changes to the website or application based on the feedback, and test it again to see if the changes have improved the user experience.

SOME ADDITIONAL RESOURCES FOR THESE PROJECTS

Build a simple computer:
PCPartPicker: https://pcpartpicker.com/
Tom's Hardware: https://www.tomshardware.com/

Design a network security plan:
NIST Cybersecurity Framework: https://www.nist.gov/cyber-framework
Cisco Networking Academy: https://www.netacad.com/courses/networking/security

Develop a cloud application:
Amazon Web Services: https://aws.amazon.com/
Microsoft Azure: https://azure.microsoft.com/
Google Cloud Platform: https://cloud.google.com/

Build an IoT device:
Arduino: https://www.arduino.cc/
Raspberry Pi: https://www.raspberrypi.org/
Adafruit: https://www.adafruit.com/

Conduct a usability test:

Nielsen Norman Group: https://www.nngroup.com/
Usability.gov: https://www.usability.gov/

NOTES FOR THE TEACHERS

One way to reinforce the practical knowledge of the subjects covered in Chapter 1 is to encourage the students to engage in hands-on activities that illustrate the concepts they have learned.

This can include building and disassembling computer hardware, installing and configuring operating systems and software, creating and managing a computer network, designing and conducting user-centred tests, and implementing security measures.

By working with the hardware, software, and systems discussed in the chapter, students can better understand the intricacies of computer science and engineering and how the different components work together to make a functioning computer system.

Additionally, engaging in practical activities can help reinforce the key takeaways and concepts covered in the chapter and make the learning experience more memorable and meaningful.

TEACHING METHOD SUGGESTIONS

It may be helpful to use the following teaching methods and activities to help students engage with the materials:

Interactive lectures: Rather than simply lecturing to students, incorporate interactive elements into your lectures. This could include asking questions and soliciting input from the class, using multimedia resources to illustrate concepts, and encouraging discussion and debate.

Hands-on activities: To help students better understand the material and provide opportunities for hands-on learning. This could include lab exercises, programming projects, or interactive simulations.

Case studies: Use case studies to illustrate real-world applications of the concepts covered in the chapter. For example, you could discuss how cloud computing has been used in various industries or how edge computing is being used in smart homes.

Group projects: Encourage students to work in groups to complete projects that require them to apply the knowledge they have learned. For example, you could assign a project where students build a basic computer system or design a new cloud-based application.

Reflection and self-assessment: Encourage students to reflect on their own learning and provide opportunities for self-assessment. This could include journaling, peer reviews, or self-evaluations.

Guest speakers: Consider inviting guest speakers from industry or academia to speak to your class. This can allow students to learn from experts in the field and gain insights into real-world applications of the material.

COURSE MATERIALS PREPARATION

If you need suggestions for course materials preparation, I suggest to the keep the following topics in mind:
- Introduction to Computer Systems
- What is a Computer System?
- Components of a Computer System
- Computer Architectures and Systems
- Basic Computer Networking
- Network Architecture and Protocols
- Network Security and Cryptography
- Cloud Computing
- Cloud Deployment Models
- Benefits and Drawbacks of Cloud Computing
- Edge Computing
- Advantages over Traditional Cloud Computing
- Use Cases and Examples of Edge Computing

- Usability and Interaction
- Basics of User-Centered Design
- Principles of Human-Computer Interaction
- Usability Testing and Evaluation
- User Experience (UX) Design
- Operating Systems
- Basic Concepts and Functions of Operating Systems
- Process Management and Scheduling
- Memory Management and Virtual Memory
- File Systems and Storage Management
- Security and Protection
- Abbreviations Used in Chapter 1
- Key Takeaways

Of course, you can adjust the slide headlines and content to best fit your teaching style and the needs of your students.

ONLINE RESOURCES ON CSE

Here are some free resources related to computer science and engineering:

edX: edX is a massive open online course provider that offers online courses from top universities and institutions around the world. Many of these courses are free and cover a wide range of computer science and engineering topics.
Link: https://www.edx.org/

MIT OpenCourseWare: MIT OpenCourseWare is a free and open educational resource that offers high-quality online courses from the Massachusetts Institute of Technology (MIT).
Link: https://ocw.mit.edu/index.htm

Khan Academy: Khan Academy is a non-profit educational that offers free online courses, including computer science courses.

Link: https://www.khanacademy.org/

Codecademy: Codecademy is an online learning platform offering free interactive coding courses. They cover a wide range of programming languages and technologies.

Link: https://www.codecademy.com/

GitHub: GitHub is a web-based platform that provides version control and collaborative features for software development projects. It also offers a wide range of free educational resources and tutorials.

Link: https://github.com/

Stack Overflow: Stack Overflow is a question-and-answer community for developers, and it is a great resource for finding solutions to programming problems and learning about best practices.

Link: https://stackoverflow.com/

Coursera: Coursera is another online learning platform offering top universities and institutions courses. While some courses require payment, many are available for free.

Link: https://www.coursera.org/

YouTube: YouTube offers a wealth of free educational content related to computer science and engineering, including tutorials, lectures, and how-to guides.

Link: https://www.youtube.com/

OpenAI: OpenAI is an artificial intelligence research laboratory consisting of the for-profit corporation OpenAI LP and its parent company, the non-profit OpenAI Inc. It offers a wide range of free educational resources and tutorials on artificial intelligence and machine learning.

Link: https://openai.com/

Google Code-in: Google Code-in is an annual coding competition for pre-university students aged 13 to 17. It is a great opportunity for students to learn and contribute to open source software projects.

Link: https://codein.withgoogle.com/

FURTHER READING

Here is a new list of 5 books on computer systems that are suitable for non-technical high school and 1st-year uni students:

The Hidden Language of Computer Hardware and Software
ISBN: 978-0735611313
Author: Charles Petzold
Publisher: Microsoft Press
Publication Date: October 11, 2000
Retail Price: $19.79
Brief overview: This book introduces the fundamental concepts of computer systems and how they work. The book covers topics such as binary code, machine language, operating systems, and programming languages in an accessible and engaging manner.

The Most Human Human: What Talking with Computers Teaches Us About What It Means to Be Alive
ISBN: 978-0143121447
Author: Brian Christian
Publisher: Penguin Books
Publication Date: March 27, 2012
Retail Price: $17.00
Brief overview: This book explores the relationship between humans and computers and how computer systems have changed communication and interaction. The book covers topics such as artificial intelligence, natural language processing, and machine learning in a thought-provoking and accessible way.

Digital Disconnect: How Capitalism is Turning the Internet Against Democracy"
ISBN: 978-1595588678
Author: Robert W. McChesney

Publisher: The New Press
Publication Date: April 8, 2014
Retail Price: $17.95
Brief overview: This book examines the impact of digital technologies on democracy and free speech. The book covers topics such as media ownership, censorship, and the impact of social media, critically and engagingly.

Programmed Inequality: How Britain Discarded Women Technologists and Lost Its Edge in Computing
ISBN: 978-0262535182
Author: Marie Hicks
Publisher: The MIT Press
Publication Date: October 13, 2017
Retail Price: $19.95
Brief overview: This book explores the history of computing and the role of women in developing computer systems. The book covers topics such as gender bias, workplace culture, and the impact of technological change on society, in an informative and engaging way.

The Shallows: What the Internet Is Doing to Our Brains
ISBN: 978-0393339758
Author: Nicholas Carr
Publisher: W. W. Norton & Company
Publication Date: June 6, 2011
Retail Price: $15.95
Brief overview: This book examines the impact of the internet on our cognitive abilities and the way we think. The book covers topics such as attention span, memory, and the impact of technology on our ability to learn, in an accessible and thought-provoking way.

QUESTIONS AND ANSWERS

These questions summarise all the sections above to test understanding of the Introduction of Computer Systems".

QUESTIONS

1. Define the term "processor". What is its role in a computer system? Name three types of processors and describe the differences between them.

2. What is the difference between RAM and ROM? What are some common uses of each type of memory in a computer system?

3. Describe the differences between a solid-state drive (SSD) and a hard disk drive (HDD). What are the advantages and disadvantages of each type of storage device?

4. Name three different input devices that are commonly used in computer systems. For each device, describe how it is used and what types of data it can input.

5. Describe the purpose of an operating system in a computer system. Name three different operating systems and describe the differences between them.

6. What is the purpose of a network? Name three different types of networks and describe their uses and characteristics.

7. Describe the benefits and drawbacks of using cloud computing in a business environment. Give an example of a company that uses cloud computing and describe how they use it.

8. Explain the concept of "virtual memory" in an operating system. How does it work, and what are some advantages and disadvantages of using virtual memory?

9. Name three different programming languages and describe the differences between them. Give an example of a program written in each language.
10. Describe the differences between symmetric and asymmetric encryption. Give an example of a situation where each type of encryption might be used.

ANSWERS

1. A processor is the central processing unit of a computer system, responsible for executing instructions and performing calculations. Three types of processors include central processing units (CPUs), graphics processing units (GPUs), and field-programmable gate arrays (FPGAs). CPUs are general-purpose processors used for most computing tasks, while GPUs are specialised processors used for graphics and parallel processing. FPGAs are reconfigurable processors that can be customised for specific applications.

2. RAM (random access memory) is a volatile memory used to store data and instructions temporarily. Common uses of RAM include running programs and storing temporary data, while ROM is used to store firmware, BIOS, and other low-level system software. ROM (read-only memory) is a non-volatile memory used to store instructions and data needed at startup permanently.

3. SSDs are faster and more reliable than HDDs but are generally more expensive and have lower storage capacities. HDDs are slower and less reliable than SSDs, but are generally less expensive and have higher storage capacities.

4. Examples of input devices include keyboards, mice, and touchscreens. A keyboard is used for typing text and inputting commands, a mouse is used for pointing and clicking, and a touchscreen is used for inputting commands and data by touching the screen.

5. An operating system is responsible for managing the resources and processes of a computer system and providing a user interface for interacting with the system. Examples of operating systems include Windows, MacOS, and Linux. Windows is commonly used in personal computers, MacOS is commonly used in Apple computers, and Linux is commonly used in servers and embedded systems.

6. A network is a group of interconnected devices that can communicate with each other. Three types of networks include local area networks (LANs), wide area networks (WANs), and wireless networks. LANs are used to connect devices in a small area, such as a home or office. WANs are used to connect devices over a large area, such as multiple offices or cities. Wireless networks are used to connect devices over a wireless signal, such as Wi-Fi or Bluetooth.

7. Cloud computing allows businesses to access computing resources over the Internet, such as servers, storage, and applications. The benefits of cloud computing include scalability, cost-effectiveness, and accessibility. Drawbacks of cloud computing include security risks and potential downtime. An example of a cloud computing company is Netflix, which uses Amazon Web Services to store and stream its video content.

8. Virtual memory is a feature of an operating system that allows it to use hard disk space as additional RAM when the available physical RAM is insufficient. This allows programs to run even when insufficient physical memory is available. The advantages of virtual memory include improved performance and increased capacity. Disadvantages of virtual memory include increased complexity and the possibility of decreased performance due to hard disk access times.

9. Examples of programming languages include C++, Python, and Java. C++ is a high-performance language used for system-level programming and video game development. Python is a high-

level language used for scripting, data analysis, and artificial intelligence. Java is a cross-platform language used for enterprise development and Android app development.

10. Symmetric encryption is used for data storage and transfer, while asymmetric encryption is used for secure communication and authentication. Symmetric encryption uses the same key for encryption and decryption, while asymmetric encryption uses a public key for encryption and a private key for decryption. An example of symmetric encryption is the Advanced Encryption Standard (AES), while an example of asymmetric encryption is the RSA algorithm.

PRACTICE PROBLEMS

Here is a set of practice questions to help you check your understanding of the topics covered in Chapter 1 of Introduction to Computer Systems, categorised based on the sections, with their answers:

Computer Hardware:
1. Explain the difference between RAM and ROM.
2. Name three types of input devices and three types of output devices used in computers.
3. What is a motherboard, and what components are typically found on it?
4. What is the difference between a hard disk and a solid-state drive?
5. What is an Ethernet port, and what is its function in a computer?

Operating Systems:
1. What is the role of an operating system in a computer?
2. Name three popular operating systems and describe their main features.
3. What is a file system, and how does it work?

4. What is the difference between a 32-bit and a 64-bit operating system?
5. What is virtualisation, and how is it used in operating systems?

Computer Networks:
1. What is a network and what are some examples of different types of networks?
2. What is the difference between a LAN and a WAN?
3. Explain the role of a router in a computer network.
4. What is the purpose of an IP address, and how is it used in networking?
5. What is a protocol, and how is it used in networking?

Cloud Computing:
1. What is cloud computing, and how does it work?
2. Name three popular cloud computing providers and describe their main features.
3. What is virtualization, and how is it used in cloud computing?
4. What are some advantages and disadvantages of using cloud computing?
5. What is serverless computing, and how is it used in cloud computing?

Usability and Interaction:
1. What is usability, and why is it important in computer systems?
2. Name three principles of usability and explain their importance.
3. What is user-centred design, and how is it used in computer systems?

4.   What is the difference between a graphical user interface and a command-line interface?

5.   Name three examples of computer systems that have good usability and explain what makes them effective.

ANSWERS

Computer Hardware:

1.   RAM stands for Random Access Memory, and it is a type of volatile memory that temporarily stores data that the CPU is currently working on. ROM stands for Read-Only Memory, and it is a type of non-volatile memory that stores data that cannot be modified.

2.   Input devices: keyboard, mouse, scanner. Output devices: printer, monitor, speakers.

3.   A motherboard is the main circuit board in a computer that connects all the components together. Components on a motherboard include the CPU, RAM slots, expansion slots, and various connectors for input/output devices.

4.   A hard disk drive (HDD) is a type of storage device that uses spinning disks to store and retrieve data, while a solid-state drive (SSD) uses flash memory to do the same. SSDs are generally faster and more durable than HDDs but are also more expensive.

5.   An Ethernet port is a connector on a computer that is used to connect to a wired network. Its function is to send and receive data between the computer and other devices on the network.

Operating Systems:

1.   The operating system is the software that manages the computer hardware and software resources and provides common services for computer programs. It acts as an interface between the user and the computer hardware.

2. Popular operating systems include Windows, macOS, and Linux. Windows is known for its easy use and compatibility with various software. macOS is known for its stability, security, and integration with Apple devices. Linux is known for its flexibility, customisation options, and open-source nature.

3. A file system is method operating systems use to organise and store files and directories on a storage device. It provides a way for users and applications to access and manage data on the device.

4. A 32-bit operating system can address up to 4GB of RAM, while a 64-bit operating system can address much more memory. 64-bit systems are generally faster and more efficient at processing large amounts of data.

5. Virtualisation is creating a virtual version of a computing resource, such as a server, operating system, or network. It is used in operating systems to run multiple virtual machines on a single physical machine.

Computer Networks:

1. A network is a collection of computers and other devices that are connected to share resources and communicate. Examples of networks include LANs, WANs, and the Internet.

2. The Internet is a global network of interconnected networks. A LAN, or Local Area Network, is a network that covers a small area, such as a home, office, or school. A WAN, or Wide Area Network, covers a larger geographic area, such as a city or country.

3. A router is a networking device connecting multiple networks and directing data traffic between them. It uses routing tables and protocols to determine the best data path between networks.

4. An IP address is a unique identifier assigned to each device on a network, allowing them to communicate with each other using the Internet Protocol. It is used to send and receive data between devices on a network.

5. A protocol is a set of rules and standards that dictate how devices on a network communicate with each other. Examples include TCP/IP, HTTP, and FTP.

Cloud Computing:

1. Cloud computing delivers services, such as servers, storage, databases, and software, over the internet. It allows users to access these services on-demand without needing on-site infrastructure.

2. Popular cloud computing providers include Amazon Web Services, Microsoft Azure, and Google Cloud Platform. AWS is known for its wide range of services and scalability, while Azure is known for its integration with Microsoft products and services. Google Cloud Platform is known for its machine learning and artificial intelligence capabilities.

3. Virtualisation is creating a virtual version of a computing resource, such as a server, operating system, or network. It is used in cloud computing to allow users to create and manage virtual machines on demand without physical hardware.

4. The advantages of using cloud computing include scalability, flexibility, and cost-effectiveness. Disadvantages have security concerns and potential vendor lock-in.

5. Serverless computing is a model of cloud computing where the cloud provider manages the infrastructure and automatically allocates resources as needed. It is used for applications that require high scalability and availability without requiring users to address the underlying infrastructure.

Usability and Interaction:

1. Usability refers to a computer system's ease of use and effectiveness from the user's perspective. It is important in computer systems because it affects user satisfaction, productivity, and the system's overall success.

2. Three principles of usability include learnability, feedback, and consistency. Learnability refers to the ease of learning how to use the system, feedback refers to the system providing clear and immediate responses to user actions, and consistency refers to the system's consistent design and behaviour across different applications and platforms.

3. User-centred design is an approach to designing computer systems that involves understanding the needs and preferences of the user and designing the system accordingly. It involves techniques such as user research, prototyping, and usability testing.

4. A graphical user interface (GUI) is a type of user interface that allows users to interact with the system using graphical elements such as icons and buttons. A command-line interface (CLI) is a type of user interface that requires users to type commands to interact with the system.

5. Three examples of computer systems with good usability include Apple's iPhone, Airbnb's website, and Trello's productivity tool. These systems have intuitive, easy-to-use designs, clear, immediate feedback, and consistent design and behaviour.

INTRODUCTION TO SOFTWARE ENGINEERING

INTRODUCTION TO SOFTWARE ENGINEERING

Introduction to Software Engineering refers to designing, creating, and maintaining software applications. Software engineering aims to develop high-quality software that meets the requirements of the end users within a specific timeline and budget. Software engineering is a complex and interdisciplinary field involving various topics and practices, such as programming, software design, testing, project management, etc.

Some of the main topics covered in Introduction to Software Engineering include:

- *Definition and objectives of software engineering:* This topic covers the basic definition of software engineering and its objectives and principles.
- *Evolution of software engineering:* This topic traces the history of software engineering, including the development of software development methodologies, tools, and techniques.
- *Characteristics of good software:* This topic covers the key characteristics of high-quality software, such as functionality, reliability, maintainability, usability, and more.
- *Comparison with other engineering disciplines:* This topic explores the similarities and differences between software engineering and other engineering disciplines, such as mechanical or civil engineering.

DEFINITION AND OBJECTIVES OF SOFTWARE ENGINEERING

Software engineering is the process of designing, creating, testing, and maintaining software. It is an interdisciplinary field that involves a combination of computer science, mathematics, and engineering.

Software engineering aims to produce high-quality software that meets the needs of its users and is reliable, maintainable, and scalable.

The software engineering process involves a series of steps that must be followed to ensure the software is developed correctly. These steps include requirements gathering, analysis, design, coding, testing, and maintenance. The software engineering process must be well documented and repeatable, with each step building on the previous one.

The key objectives of software engineering are to ensure that software is:

Reliability: Software is considered reliable when it performs its intended functions accurately and consistently. This means that it should be free from errors and bugs and able to handle a range of inputs and scenarios without crashing or producing incorrect results. Achieving software reliability requires careful testing and quality assurance processes, as well as the use of robust coding techniques and best practices.

Maintainability: Software should be easy to modify or update to meet changing needs over time. This includes making changes to the software code and updating its documentation and supporting materials. Maintaining software is an ongoing process that involves regular updates, bug fixes, and support for end-users who may encounter issues or require assistance with using the software.

Efficiency: Software should use computing resources efficiently to minimise cost and time. This means that it should be optimised for performance, using the least amount of computing power and memory possible while still delivering its intended functionality. Achieving software efficiency involves careful planning and design, as well as the use of efficient algorithms and programming techniques.

Usability: Software with a well-designed user interface should be easy to use and understand. This includes visual design, navigation, and accessibility for users with different needs and abilities. Achieving software usability requires careful user testing and feedback, as well as the use of user-centred design principles.

Security: Software should be designed to prevent unauthorised access and protect data. Achieving software security requires careful planning, design, encryption, authentication, and other security measures. This includes protecting against external threats such as hackers and malware and internal threats such as data breaches or unauthorised access by employees or other insiders. It also involves ongoing monitoring and updates to stay up-to-date with emerging security threats and vulnerabilities.

Scalability: Software should be designed to scale up or down to handle changing workloads or user demand. This includes considerations such as performance under heavy load, support for distributed systems, and the ability to add or remove computing resources as needed. Achieving software scalability requires careful planning and design and the use of scalable architectures and infrastructure.

Interoperability: Software should be designed to work seamlessly with other software and systems, including those developed by different vendors or using different technologies. This includes data exchange formats, APIs, and integration with third-party systems. Achieving software interoperability requires careful planning and design and adherence to relevant standards and best practices.

Accessibility: Software should be designed to be accessible to users with different needs and abilities, including those with disabilities or impairments. Achieving software accessibility requires careful testing and feedback from users with different needs and abilities, as well as the use of inclusive design principles. This includes support for assistive technologies, accessible user interfaces, and compliance with accessibility guidelines and standards.

Compliance: Software should be designed to comply with relevant laws, regulations, and industry standards. This includes data privacy regulations, cybersecurity standards, and ethical considerations. Achieving software compliance requires careful planning and design, as well as ongoing monitoring and updates to stay up-to-date with changes to regulations and standards.

Software engineering aims to design and develop functional, safe, useable, efficient and maintained software for its intended audience.

EVOLUTION OF SOFTWARE ENGINEERING

The evolution of software engineering refers to the changes and advancements in software engineering over time. This includes the development of software development methodologies, tools, and techniques, as well as the evolution of the software industry and the role of software in society. Understanding the evolution of software engineering is essential for anyone working in the field, as it provides insight into how the area has developed and how it may continue to evolve.

The evolution of software engineering can be traced back to the late 1950s and early 1960s when the first software engineering conference was held. Software development was a relatively new field at that time, and developers were still learning how to write and manage software effectively.

Over the years, software engineering has undergone significant changes and improvements, driven by the need to address increasingly complex software systems and the challenges associated with developing and maintaining them.

Some key milestones in the evolution of software engineering include:

Waterfall Model: The Waterfall Model was one of the first software development methodologies developed in the 1970s. It is a sequential approach to software development, with distinct phases for requirements gathering, design, implementation, testing, and maintenance. In this model, each phase must be completed before moving on to the next, which can make it difficult to make changes later in the development process. However, it can be useful for projects with well-defined requirements and a clear understanding of the final product.

Agile Software Development: Agile software development emerged in the 1990s as a response to the limitations of the Waterfall Model. It emphasises flexibility, collaboration, and rapid iteration, focusing on delivering working software quickly and continuously. In Agile development, the emphasis is on working closely with customers and stakeholders and adapting to changing requirements and priorities over time. This approach can be more adaptable and responsive to evolving needs but may require ongoing communication and management.

Object-Oriented Programming: Object-oriented programming (OOP) is a programming paradigm developed in the 1980s that has become a cornerstone of modern software development. OOP emphasises the creation of reusable software components, making it easier to develop and maintain large software systems. In OOP, the software is structured around objects that represent real-world entities, with data and behaviour encapsulated within each object. This approach can help make the software more modular, flexible, and easier to maintain over time.

Open Source Software: Open source software refers to software that is developed and distributed under an open-source license, which allows developers to access, modify, and distribute the software freely. The open-source model can help to foster innovation, collaboration, and community involvement in software development. Open-source software has become a key component of many software systems, particularly in web development.

DevOps: DevOps is a set of practices emphasising collaboration and communication between development and operations teams to deliver software quickly and reliably. It includes tools and techniques for automating software development, testing, and deployment processes. The DevOps approach can help reduce the time and cost involved in software development while improving the quality and reliability of the software produced.

Rapid Application Development (RAD): Rapid Application Development is a software development methodology that emerged in the 1980s and 1990s. It emphasises iterative development, prototyping, and user feedback, focusing on quickly delivering working software. RAD can be useful for projects with rapidly changing requirements or for creating prototypes or proof-of-concept software.

Test-Driven Development (TDD): Test-Driven Development is a programming technique that emphasises writing automated tests before writing the software code. The idea is to ensure that the software meets the specified requirements and behaves correctly before moving on to further development. TDD can help reduce the number of bugs and errors in software and encourage more modular and reusable code.

Continuous Integration/Continuous Delivery (CI/CD): Continuous Integration and Continuous Delivery aim to streamline software development by automating build, testing, and deployment processes. CI/CD can help reduce the time and cost involved in software development while improving the quality and reliability of the software produced. It involves frequent and ongoing integration and testing of code changes, with a focus on quickly delivering working software to end-users.

Cloud Computing: Cloud computing is a technology that enables the delivery of computing services over the Internet rather than through on-site hardware and infrastructure. Cloud computing has revolutionised how software is developed and deployed by providing on-demand scalable and flexible computing resources. Cloud computing can help reduce the cost and complexity of software development and enable more efficient collaboration and communication between developers and stakeholders.

These milestones and others have contributed to the evolution of software engineering and have helped make it the sophisticated field it is today. As technology continues to advance, we can expect further expansion in software engineering, with new tools, techniques, and methodologies emerging to address the challenges of developing and maintaining complex software systems.

CHARACTERISTICS OF GOOD SOFTWARE

Characteristics of good software refer to the qualities that make software effective, efficient, reliable, maintainable, and usable.

Some of the key characteristics of good software include the following:

Functionality: Good software should be able to perform the tasks for which it was designed effectively and efficiently. This means that the software should be able to accomplish its intended goals with a focus on meeting the needs of its users. Achieving software functionality requires careful planning, design, regular testing, and user feedback.

Reliability: Reliability and consistent performance under varying settings and inputs are hallmarks of high-quality software. Reliable software results from rigorous testing, quality assurance procedures, and best practices in code construction. This means that there shouldn't be any hiccups or inaccurate outputs in the event of an unexpected situation, and the software should be bug-free.

Usability: Good software with a clear and intuitive interface should be easy to use and understand by its intended users. This means that the software should be designed with user needs and preferences in mind, focusing on usability, accessibility, and user experience design. Achieving software usability requires careful user testing and feedback, as well as the use of user-centred design principles.

Efficiency: Good software should use computing resources effectively and efficiently without unnecessary overhead. This means the software should be optimised for performance, using the least computing power and memory possible while still delivering its intended functionality. Achieving software efficiency involves careful planning and design, as well as the use of efficient algorithms and programming techniques.

Maintainability: Good software should be easy to maintain and update, with clear and modular code that can be easily modified and extended. This means the software should be designed with maintainability in mind, focusing on code readability, documentation, and version control. Achieving software maintainability requires careful planning and design, as well as the use of best practices for software development and maintenance.

Portability: Good software should be able to run on multiple platforms and operating systems without requiring significant modifications. This means that the software should be designed with portability in mind, using open standards and protocols that can be easily adapted to different environments. Achieving software portability requires careful planning, design, and regular testing and validation across different platforms and systems.

Security: Good software should be designed to protect against security threats and vulnerabilities and ensure user data's privacy and integrity. Achieving software security requires careful planning, design, and ongoing monitoring and updates to stay up-to-date with emerging security threats and vulnerabilities. This means the software should be developed with security, encryption, authentication, and other security measures to protect against unauthorised access and data breaches.

Scalability: Good software should be designed to handle increasing amounts of data and users without sacrificing performance or reliability. This means the software should be developed with scalability in mind, using scalable architectures and infrastructure that can adapt easily to changing needs over time. Achieving software scalability requires careful planning, design, and regular testing and validation under varying workloads and scenarios.

Testability: Good software should be designed with testing in mind, with clear and verifiable requirements, test cases, and quality metrics. This means that the software should be developed with a focus on testability, using testing frameworks and tools to automate testing and ensure software quality. Achieving software testability requires careful planning and design, as well as the use of testing best practices and techniques.

Interoperability: Good software should be able to interact and communicate effectively with other software and systems, using open standards and protocols. This means that the software should be developed with interoperability in mind, using standards-based interfaces and data exchange formats that can be easily integrated with other.

Adaptability: Good software should be designed to adapt to changing requirements and environments over time. This means that the software should be developed with adaptability in mind, using flexible architectures and infrastructure that can be easily modified or extended as needed.

Accessibility: Good software should be designed to be accessible to users with different needs and abilities, including those with disabilities or impairments. This means the software should be developed with accessibility in mind, using accessible user interfaces, support for assistive technologies, and compliance with accessibility guidelines and standards.

Resilience: Good software should be designed to resist failures and disruptions, with built-in redundancy and failover mechanisms. This means that the software should be developed with resilience, using fault-tolerant architectures and disaster recovery plans to ensure business continuity and data integrity.

Transparency: Good software should be designed to be transparent, with clear documentation and traceability of development processes and decision-making. This means that the software should be developed with transparency in mind, using open and collaborative development processes involving regular communication and stakeholder feedback.

Sustainability: Good software should be designed to be sustainable over the long term, focusing on reducing environmental impact and resource usage. This means that the software should be developed with sustainability in mind, using energy-efficient computing and infrastructure and considering the environmental impact of the software throughout its lifecycle.

To ensure that software exhibits these characteristics, software engineers use various methodologies and techniques such as agile development, test-driven development, code reviews, and software quality assurance. Additionally, software engineering best practices involve continuous improvement and iteration to ensure that software remains effective and relevant.

COMPARISON WITH OTHER ENGINEERING DISCIPLINES

Software engineering is designed and developed to solve problems or meet specific requirements. This process differs in several ways from traditional engineering disciplines such as civil, mechanical, or electrical engineering.

Firstly, software engineering is a relatively new field that has emerged in response to the growing importance of software in our lives. Traditional engineering disciplines have existed for much longer and have well-established practices and standards.

Secondly, software engineering is a highly collaborative field that involves teams of developers, designers, and other professionals working together to build software. This differs from traditional engineering disciplines, which often involve individual work or small groups.

Thirdly, software engineering is a rapidly changing field that requires constant learning and adaptation to new technologies and practices. This differs from traditional engineering disciplines, which tend to be more stable and predictable.

Finally, software engineering is a field that is heavily influenced by the business and commercial aspects of software development. This is different from traditional engineering disciplines, which are often more focused on research and development.

Despite these differences, software engineering shares many similarities with traditional engineering disciplines. Both fields involve the application of science and mathematics to solve complex problems and both require a rigorous approach to problem-solving and testing.

Overall, software engineering is a unique and dynamic field that requires a combination of technical, creative, and business skills to succeed.

PRACTICE QUESTIONS

1. What is software engineering, and how does it differ from other engineering disciplines?
2. What are the key objectives of software engineering, and why are they important?
3. What are some of the key milestones in the evolution of software engineering, and how have they influenced the way software is developed today?
4. What are the key characteristics of good software, and why are they important for ensuring software quality?
5. How does software engineering relate to other areas of computer science, such as programming, algorithms, and data structures?
6. What are some of the key challenges facing software engineering today, and how are they being addressed?
7. How has the rise of open-source software impacted the field of software engineering, and what are some of the benefits and drawbacks of open-source development?
8. What are some of the key differences between traditional software development methodologies like Waterfall and more modern approaches like Agile?
9. How have cloud computing and other new technologies impacted how software is developed and deployed today?

10. What are some of the key ethical and social considerations surrounding software engineering, and how can engineers ensure their work is ethical and responsible?

KEY TAKEAWAYS

- Software engineering is a discipline that involves applying engineering principles and practices to developing software systems, focusing on meeting the needs of users and stakeholders.
- The key objectives of software engineering are to ensure that software is reliable, maintainable, efficient, usable, secure, testable, scalable, interoperable, and portable.
- The evolution of software engineering has been shaped by various factors, including advances in computer hardware and software, changing user needs and expectations, and new software development methodologies and practices.
- Good software should be functional, reliable, usable, efficient, maintainable, portable, secure, testable, scalable, interoperable, adaptable, transparent, and sustainable to ensure that it meets the needs of its users and performs its intended functions accurately and consistently.
- Software engineering is closely related to other areas of computer science, such as programming, algorithms, data structures, and computer networks.
- Some of the key challenges facing software engineering today include managing software complexity, ensuring software security and privacy, adapting to changing requirements and environments, and developing software accessible to users with different needs and abilities.
- Open-source software has significantly impacted software engineering, enabling greater collaboration and innovation while posing potential security and licensing issues.

- Traditional software development methodologies like Waterfall tend to be more linear and sequential, while more modern approaches like Agile tend to be more iterative and flexible.
- The emergence of cloud computing and other new technologies have impacted how software is developed and deployed today, providing scalable and flexible computing resources on demand.
- Software engineers have an ethical and social responsibility to ensure their work is honest, responsible, and transparent by following ethical codes of conduct, engaging in ongoing training and education, and being collaborative and communicative in their development processes.

ANSWERS TO PRACTICE QUESTIONS

1. Software engineering is a discipline that involves applying engineering principles and practices to developing software systems. It differs from other engineering disciplines because software systems are typically intangible and more flexible than physical ones. They often involve complex interactions with users and other software systems.

2. The key objectives of software engineering are to ensure that software is reliable, maintainable, efficient, usable, secure, testable, scalable, interoperable, and portable. These objectives are important because they help to ensure that software meets the needs of its users, performs its intended functions accurately and consistently, and can be adapted to changing requirements and environments over time.

3. Some key milestones in the evolution of software engineering include the development of the Waterfall model, the emergence of Agile software development, the rise of open-source software, and the increasing adoption of cloud computing and other new technologies. These milestones have influenced how software is developed today by promoting more collaborative, iterative, and flexible approaches to software development.

4. The key characteristics of good software include functionality, reliability, usability, efficiency, maintainability, portability, security, testability, scalability, interoperability, adaptability, transparency, and sustainability. These characteristics are essential for ensuring software quality, as they help to ensure that software meets the needs of its users, performs its intended functions accurately and consistently, and can be adapted to changing requirements and environments over time.

5. Software engineering relates to other areas of computer science, such as programming, algorithms, and data structures. These concepts and techniques are used to design, implement, test, and maintain software systems that meet specific requirements and goals.

6. Some key challenges facing software engineering today include managing software complexity, ensuring software security and privacy, adapting to changing requirements and environments, and developing software accessible to users with different needs and abilities. These challenges are being addressed through various approaches, such as using modular and scalable architectures, automated testing and deployment, and adopting ethical and sustainable software development practices.

7. The rise of open-source software has impacted the field of software engineering by enabling developers to access, modify, and distribute software freely. Some benefits of open-source development include greater collaboration and innovation, while some drawbacks include potential security and licensing issues.

8. Traditional software development methodologies like Waterfall tend to be more linear and sequential, with distinct requirements gathering, design, implementation, testing, and maintenance phases. More modern approaches like Agile tend to be more iterative and flexible, focusing on delivering working software quickly and continuously through collaboration and feedback from users and stakeholders.

9. The emergence of cloud computing and other new technologies have impacted how software is developed and deployed today by providing scalable and flexible computing resources on demand. This has enabled software engineers to develop and deploy software more quickly and efficiently, improving collaboration and communication between developers and stakeholders.

10. Some of the key ethical and social considerations surrounding software engineering include issues related to privacy, security, accessibility, bias, and sustainability. Software engineers can ensure their work is honest and responsible by adopting ethical codes of conduct, engaging in ongoing training and education, and being transparent and collaborative in their development processes.

PROJECT WORK

Here is a list of project work that students can conduct to enrich their knowledge in this software engineering introduction section.

Project - 1: Develop a simple software application using Agile methodology. Students could work in small teams to develop a basic software application using Agile methodology, focusing on frequent collaboration, feedback, and iteration. This could involve creating user stories, designing and implementing software features, testing and debugging the software, and presenting the final product to the class.

Project – 2: Conduct a software quality analysis on an existing application. Students could select an existing software application and conduct a qualitative analysis to evaluate its functionality, reliability, usability, efficiency, maintainability, portability, security, testability, scalability, and interoperability. This could involve using testing tools and techniques to identify potential issues and proposing solutions for improving the software's quality.

Project – 3: Compare and contrast Waterfall and Agile development methodologies. Students could research and compare the Waterfall and Agile development methodologies and present their findings to the class in the form of a written report, a presentation, or a debate. This could involve discussing the strengths and weaknesses of each methodology and identifying situations where one approach may be more appropriate than the other.

Project – 4: Develop a software project plan using project management tools. Students could use project management tools such as Gantt charts, resource allocation tables, and risk management matrices to develop a project plan for a hypothetical software development project. This could involve identifying project goals and requirements, creating a project schedule, allocating resources, and identifying potential risks and mitigation strategies.

Project – 5: Create an open-source software project. Students could collaborate to create an open-source software project using tools and platforms like GitHub and GitLab. This could involve selecting a software idea, designing and implementing the software, testing and debugging the software, and publishing the software as an open-source project for others to use and contribute to.

PROJECT SUPPORT

1. *Develop a simple software application using Agile methodology:*
   - Clearly define the scope and goals of the project, and break them down into smaller, more manageable tasks or user stories.
   - Establish a clear communication plan and project timeline to ensure everyone on the team is on the same page.
   - Use project management tools like Kanban boards or Scrum boards to track progress, identify bottlenecks, and ensure that work is distributed evenly among team members.

- Prioritise testing and feedback throughout the development process to identify potential issues early and make iterative improvements to the software.
- Have regular team meetings to discuss progress, challenges, and successes and celebrate milestones and achievements together.

2. ***Conduct a software quality analysis on an existing application:***
   - Clearly define the quality criteria you will be evaluating, such as functionality, reliability, usability, efficiency, maintainability, portability, security, testability, scalability, and interoperability.
   - Use a variety of testing tools and techniques, such as manual testing, automated testing, and performance testing, to identify potential issues and evaluate the software against the quality criteria.
   - Document your findings and propose potential solutions for improving the software's quality based on your analysis.

3. ***Compare and contrast Waterfall and Agile development methodologies:***
   - Research and gather information on the Waterfall and Agile development methodologies, including their strengths, weaknesses, and key characteristics.
   - Clearly define the scope and objectives of your comparison, and establish a clear framework or structure for your analysis.
   - Use examples and case studies to illustrate the similarities and differences between the two methodologies and highlight situations where one approach may be more appropriate.
   - Encourage constructive debate and discussion among team members, and be open to different perspectives and opinions.

4. ***Develop a software project plan using project management tools:***
   - Clearly define the goals and scope of the project, and break them down into smaller, more manageable tasks or milestones.
   - Use project management tools like Gantt charts, resource allocation tables, and risk management matrices to establish a clear project timeline, allocate resources, and identify potential risks and mitigation strategies.
   - Be flexible and adaptive, and be prepared to adjust your project plan as needed in response to changing requirements or constraints.
   - Communicate regularly with team members, stakeholders, and project sponsors to ensure everyone knows project progress, challenges, and successes.

5. ***Create an open-source software project:***
   - Clearly define the goals and scope of the project, and select a software idea that aligns with your team's interests and skills.
   - Establish clear guidelines and standards for code quality, documentation, and collaboration to ensure that the project is accessible and usable by others.
   - Use tools and platforms like GitHub and GitLab to manage version control, track issues and bugs, and collaborate with other contributors.
   - Encourage feedback and contributions from other users and contributors, and be open to incorporating new ideas and perspectives into the project.
   - Celebrate successes and milestones, and use the project to develop your skills, network with other developers, and contribute to the broader open-source community.

FURTHER READING

Here are some books on software engineering that are suitable for non-technical students:

"Software Engineering: A Practitioner's Approach" by Roger Pressman - This book is a comprehensive introduction to software engineering that covers all the key concepts and practices, including software requirements, design, testing, and maintenance. The book is written in an accessible, easy-to-understand style, and includes numerous examples and case studies.

"The Mythical Man-Month: Essays on Software Engineering" by Frederick Brooks - This classic book is a collection of essays on software engineering written by a pioneer in the field. The book covers topics such as project management, software design, and programming languages and provides valuable insights into the challenges and complexities of software development.

"Clean Code: A Handbook of Agile Software Craftsmanship" by Robert Martin - This book is a practical guide to writing clean, well-designed code that is easy to maintain and understand. The book covers topics such as code quality, testing, refactoring, and design patterns and provides numerous examples and case studies to illustrate the concepts.

"Head First Software Development" by Dan Pilone and Russ Miles - This book is a beginner-friendly introduction to software development that covers all the key concepts and practices, including requirements gathering, design, coding, testing, and deployment. The book is written in a fun, engaging style, with plenty of visuals and examples to help readers understand the material.

"The Pragmatic Programmer: From Journeyman to Master" by Andrew Hunt and David Thomas - This book is a practical guide to becoming a better software developer, covering topics such as coding practices, testing, debugging, and team collaboration. The book is written in a conversational, easy-to-read style, with plenty of real-world examples and case studies to illustrate the concepts.

The above books provide a solid introduction to software engineering concepts and practices and are written in a style that is accessible and engaging for non-technical students.

ONLINE RESOURCES

Khan Academy's "Computer Science" course - This free online course covers various computer science topics, including programming, algorithms, data structures, and software engineering. The course is designed for beginners and briefly introduces the material.

Coursera's "Software Engineering Essentials" course - This course is aimed at beginners who are interested in learning about software engineering. It covers requirements gathering, software design, testing, and project management. The course is self-paced and includes video lectures, quizzes, and assignments.

Codecademy's "Learn Software Engineering" course - This free online course covers the basics of software engineering, including project management, version control, testing, and deployment. The course includes interactive lessons and hands-on coding exercises.

edX's "Software Development Fundamentals" course - This course covers the basics of software development, including software design, coding, testing, and debugging. The self-paced course includes video lectures, quizzes, and coding assignments.

GitHub's "Introduction to Software Engineering" guide introduces software engineering concepts and practices, including version control, collaboration, testing, and deployment. The guide includes interactive tutorials and examples and is suitable for beginners new to software development.

The above online resources provide a variety of ways for non-technical students to learn about software engineering concepts and practices, including interactive tutorials, video lectures, quizzes, and coding exercises.

COMPUTER SYSTEM ENGINEERING

Computer system engineering involves designing, developing, testing, and evaluating computer systems, including hardware and software components. It requires a strong understanding of computer architecture, operating systems, programming languages, and other related technologies. Computer system engineers work to optimise computer system performance and functionality, ensure system security and reliability, and meet end-users needs.

Some of the main areas of focus in computer system engineering include:

- Computer hardware design and development, including designing and developing computer systems, components, and peripherals.
- Operating system design and optimisation, including designing and developing operating systems that manage computer resources.
- Network design and optimisation, including designing and developing networks that connect computer systems to each other and to the Internet.
- Software engineering and development, including designing, developing, and testing software applications.
- Embedded systems design and development, including designing and developing computer systems that are integrated into other devices or systems.
- Cybersecurity and information assurance, including designing and implementing security measures to protect computer systems and data from cyber-attacks.
- Human-computer interaction (HCI), including designing and developing interfaces between computer systems and human users.

- Distributed computing involves designing and developing systems that consist of multiple computers that work together to perform tasks, which is also an important area of computer system engineering.
- Robotics and Cybernetics are related to computer-controlled systems, and their design and development can also fall under the domain of computer system engineering.
- Embedded systems involve designing and developing computer systems that are integrated into other devices or systems, such as cars or medical equipment, which is also a part of computer system engineering.
- Computer graphics and visualisation involve designing and developing software and hardware systems that create, display, and manipulate visual images, which is an essential area of computer system engineering.
- Medical image computing involves developing software and hardware systems for medical imaging and analysis, which is a specialised area of computer system engineering.
- Computer and network security involves designing and developing systems and strategies to protect computer systems and networks from unauthorised access or attacks, which is also an important area of computer system engineering.

Computer system engineers may work on various projects, including designing and developing computer hardware and software systems, implementing network infrastructure, and developing new technologies and applications. They may work in various industries, including computer and electronics manufacturing, software development, telecommunications, and defence.

In addition to technical skills, computer system engineers also need strong problem-solving and critical thinking skills and the ability to work collaboratively with other engineers and stakeholders. They must also stay up-to-date with the latest technological advancements and be willing to learn and adapt to new tools and techniques continuously.

COMPONENTS OF A COMPUTER SYSTEM

Components of a computer system are the hardware and software components that work together to perform tasks and process data.

The hardware components include the following:

Central Processing Unit (CPU): The CPU is the computer's brain, responsible for executing instructions and performing calculations. It controls the other hardware components and runs the software programs.

Random Access Memory (RAM): RAM is a temporary memory that stores data and programs currently used by the computer. It allows the computer to quickly access and manipulate data, but it is lost when it is turned off.

Hard Disk Drive (HDD) or Solid-State Drive (SSD): These storage devices store data and programs permanently. The HDD is a traditional storage device that uses spinning disks to read and write data, while the SSD is a newer type of storage device that uses flash memory to store data.

Input/Output (I/O) devices: These devices are used to enter data into the computer or display the results of computations, such as monitors, keyboards, mice, and printers.

Graphics Processing Unit (GPU): The GPU is a specialised processor responsible for rendering images and graphics. It offloads some of the processing work from the CPU, allowing for faster and more efficient rendering of images and videos.

Motherboard: The motherboard is the computer system's main circuit board that connects all components.

The software components of a computer system include the following:

Operating System (OS): The OS is a software program that manages the computer's hardware and provides application services and interfaces.

Application Software: Application software performs specific tasks, such as word processing, spreadsheets, and multimedia applications.

System Software: System software provides a platform for other software to run on, such as compilers, interpreters, and drivers.

Programming Software: Programming software is used to create other software, such as compilers, debuggers, and integrated development environments (IDEs).

The hardware components of a computer system are responsible for physically performing tasks and processing data. In contrast, the software components provide the instructions and interfaces necessary to control the hardware and complete tasks. The components work together to allow the computer to perform various tasks and functions, from basic word processing to complex simulations and calculations.

OPERATING SYSTEMS AND SYSTEM SOFTWARE

Operating systems (OS) and system software are critical components of computer systems. An operating system is a software that acts as a mediator between hardware and application software. It manages the computer system's resources, including the CPU, memory, and input/output devices, and provides a platform for running applications.

The primary functions of an operating system include process management, memory management, file systems and storage management, and security and protection. Process management involves managing multiple processes running simultaneously on the system, allocating resources to each process and scheduling them for execution. Memory management involves managing memory allocation and deallocation, providing virtual memory, and ensuring the system has enough memory for all the running processes.

File systems and storage management manage files and storage devices such as hard disk drives, solid-state drives, and optical drives. This includes maintaining a file hierarchy, managing access permissions, and managing storage allocation and deallocation.

Security and protection are critical aspects of operating systems, especially in today's world, where cyber attacks are a significant threat. Operating systems provide features such as encryption, firewalls, and antivirus software to protect against various forms of attacks, including viruses, malware, and unauthorised access.

In addition to operating systems, there are other types of the system software, such as device drivers, which allow the operating system to communicate with hardware devices, and utility software, which provides various tools for managing and optimising the computer system.

APPLICATION SOFTWARE

Application software is computer software designed to help users perform specific tasks. It differs from system software, which manages and controls computer hardware and other software programs. Application software can be further categorised into different types, including:

Productivity software: This application software is designed to help users perform productivity-related tasks, such as creating and editing documents, spreadsheets, and presentations. Examples include Microsoft Office, Google Docs, and LibreOffice.

Multimedia software: This application software is designed to help users create, edit, and view multimedia content, such as images, audio, and video. Examples include Adobe Photoshop, Audacity, and VLC Media Player.

Communication software: This application software is designed to help users communicate with others over a network, such as email, messaging, and video conferencing software. Examples include Team, Zoom, and Slack.

Educational software: This application software is designed to help users learn and improve their skills and knowledge. Examples include language learning software, math games, and educational videos.

Entertainment software: This application software is designed to provide users with entertainment and leisure activities, such as games, music players, and streaming services. Examples include Netflix, Spotify, and Steam.

DISTRIBUTED SYSTEMS AND NETWORKING

Distributed systems refer to a group of computers that work together as a single system to provide a standard set of services or functions. In a distributed system, the computers are connected through a network and communicate to share resources, coordinate tasks, and manage data.

One of the most common examples of distributed computing is using a distributed computing system to perform complex scientific calculations or simulations. For example, the SETI@home project uses a distributed computing system to search for extraterrestrial life by analysing radio telescope data. Volunteers worldwide download a small software program that uses their computers' idle processing power to analyse data from the telescope. The collective processing power of all the computers in the distributed system allows scientists to perform calculations that would be impossible to perform on a single computer.

Another example of distributed computing is cloud computing, which involves using distributed computing resources over the internet. Cloud computing allows users to access computing resources, such as processing power, storage, and applications, on-demand and pay only for what they use. Cloud computing is used in a wide range of applications, from web-based services and e-commerce to big data analytics and machine learning.

Distributed computing is also used in the development of distributed applications, where different components of an application may be running on different computers or devices. For example, a web-based application may use a distributed database to store data, with different servers responsible for different parts of the database.

Networking is the process of connecting two or more computing devices to share resources and information. Networking can be done using various hardware and software technologies, including local area networks (LANs), wide area networks (WANs), and the Internet.

Networking refers to connecting computers and other devices to share resources and communicate with each other. Computer networks can be classified based on their geographic scopes, such as local area networks (LANs), metropolitan area networks (MANs), and wide area networks (WANs). They can also be classified based on their topologies, such as bus, ring, star, and mesh topologies.

Networking protocols define the rules for communication between devices on a network. Some standard networking protocols include the Transmission Control Protocol/Internet Protocol (TCP/IP), User Datagram Protocol (UDP), Simple Mail Transfer Protocol (SMTP), Hypertext Transfer Protocol (HTTP), and Secure Sockets Layer (SSL). Some specific topics related to distributed systems and networking include network architecture and protocols, network security and cryptography, distributed computing, and cloud computing. Understanding these topics is essential for building and managing modern computer systems capable of handling the demands of today's digital world.

ROBOTICS AND CYBERNETICS

Robotics and cybernetics are two closely related fields that involve designing, constructing, and operating robots and other intelligent machines.

Robotics is the study of programmed machines that can carry out tasks autonomously or with human guidance. Robotics involves the integration of various technologies, such as mechanical engineering, electrical engineering, and computer science, to design and build robots that can perform specific tasks. The primary goal of robotics is to create intelligent machines that can operate independently and efficiently in various settings.

Cybernetics focuses on the interaction between machines and their environment and the feedback loops that enable the machines to adapt to changing conditions. On the other hand, cybernetics studies the control and communication systems in machines and living organisms. It involves the application of mathematical and engineering principles to understand and design systems that can regulate their own behaviour.

Examples of applications of robotics and cybernetics include:

- *Industrial robots:* These are robots used in manufacturing processes to automate repetitive and dangerous tasks such as welding, painting, and assembly.
- *Medical robots:* These are robots used in healthcare settings for surgical procedures, physical therapy, and patient monitoring.
- *Autonomous vehicles:* These are vehicles equipped with sensors and control systems that enable them to navigate without human intervention. Examples include self-driving cars and drones.
- *Humanoid robots:* These are robots that resemble humans in appearance and are designed to perform tasks that require human-

like dexterity and movement, such as working in hazardous environments or assisting people with disabilities.

- **Control systems:** These are systems used to regulate the behaviour of machines, such as the cruise control system in a car, which regulates the vehicle's speed based on feedback from sensors.

Robotics and cybernetics involve designing, constructing, and operating intelligent machines and systems that can perform tasks autonomously or with human guidance. They have numerous applications in various industries, including manufacturing, healthcare, transportation, and entertainment.

EMBEDDED SYSTEMS

Embedded systems refer to computer systems designed to perform specific functions and are embedded within a larger system. These systems can be found in various devices, including cars, medical devices, home appliances, and industrial machinery.

Embedded systems typically consist of a microcontroller, a small computer chip containing a central processing unit (CPU), memory, and input/output (I/O) peripherals. The microcontroller is programmed to perform specific tasks and is often embedded within a larger electronic system.

Examples of embedded systems include:

- **Automotive systems:** Modern cars contain numerous embedded systems, including systems for engine control, braking, airbags, and entertainment.
- **Medical devices:** Medical devices such as pacemakers and insulin pumps contain embedded systems that regulate patient care and monitor vital signs.

- *Home appliances:* Many home appliances, such as washing machines, refrigerators, and air conditioners, contain embedded systems that regulate their operation.
- *Industrial machinery:* Embedded systems monitor and control various processes, such as assembly lines, packaging machines, and conveyor belts.

Developing embedded systems requires a strong understanding of computer architecture, electronics, and programming. Embedded systems engineers must consider power consumption, reliability, and real-time response factors when designing these systems.

COMPUTER GRAPHICS AND VISUALISATION

Computer graphics and visualisation involve creating, manipulating, and rendering visual content using computer software and hardware. It encompasses various applications, from creating video games and special effects in movies to designing visualisations for scientific data and virtual reality environments.

Computer graphics involve creating and manipulating images and animations using computer software. This can include 2D and 3D graphics, vector graphics, and raster graphics. Some popular computer graphics applications include video game development, animation, graphic design, and visual effects in movies and TV shows.

On the other hand, visualisation involves using computer software to create visual representations of data. This can include charts, graphs, maps, and other interactive visualisations that help users better understand complex data. Visualisation techniques can be used in various fields, including science, engineering, finance, and healthcare.

Some examples of computer graphics and visualisation applications include:

- Creating video games with realistic 3D graphics and animations.

- Developing special effects for movies and TV shows using computer-generated imagery (CGI).
- Designing and animating characters for animated movies and TV shows.
- Creating virtual reality environments for gaming, education, and training purposes.
- Developing data visualisations to help scientists better understand complex data in astronomy, biology, and physics fields.
- Creating interactive visualisations for financial data, such as stock market trends and economic indicators.
- Developing user interfaces with 2D and 3D graphics for applications like video editing software and photo editing tools.
- Overall, computer graphics and visualisation are important areas of computer science that allow for creating engaging and informative visual content.

MEDICAL IMAGE COMPUTING (MIC)

Medical Image Computing (MIC) refers to the use of computer algorithms and techniques to analyse, interpret, and visualise medical images. It is an interdisciplinary field that combines computer science, physics, mathematics, engineering, and medicine to develop and apply new imaging technologies and tools for medical diagnosis, treatment planning, and research.

Medical imaging modalities include X-ray, computed tomography (CT), magnetic resonance imaging (MRI), ultrasound, and positron emission tomography (PET). MIC focuses on developing algorithms and techniques to process and analyze the images generated by these modalities.

Some examples of applications of MIC include:

- **Segmentation and analysis of medical images:** Segmentation refers to separating an image into multiple regions or objects of interest. In medical imaging, segmentation identifies and isolates specific structures or abnormalities, such as tumours, blood vessels, or brain regions. MIC algorithms are used to develop segmentation methods that can accurately and efficiently process large volumes of medical images.

- **Image registration:** Image registration is the process of aligning two or more images to enable comparison or combination of information. MIC algorithms can be used to develop image registration methods that can accurately align images acquired from different modalities, such as MRI and CT, or from different time points, to monitor disease progression or treatment response.

- **Computer-aided diagnosis:** MIC algorithms can be used to develop computer-aided diagnosis systems to assist physicians in interpreting medical images. For example, algorithms can automatically detect and quantify features associated with a disease or condition, such as bone density in osteoporosis or brain atrophy in Alzheimer's disease.

- **Virtual and augmented reality: MIC** techniques can be used to develop virtual and augmented reality systems that provide physicians with immersive and interactive 3D visualisations of medical images. These systems can help physicians better understand complex anatomy and plan surgical procedures.

- **Image-guided therapy:** MIC algorithms can be used to develop image-guided therapy systems that use medical images to guide minimally invasive procedures, such as biopsy or ablation. These systems can help physicians to precisely target the area of interest and avoid damaging surrounding healthy tissue.

MIC is an important field that can improve medical diagnosis, treatment, and research by providing physicians with better image analysis, interpretation, and visualisation tools.

COMPUTER AND NETWORK SECURITY

Computer and network security is an essential aspect of computer systems engineering. It protects computer systems and networks from unauthorised access, theft, damage, and disruption. There are various types of computer and network security threats, including viruses, malware, hacking, phishing, and identity theft.

Computer and network security professionals work to identify potential vulnerabilities and develop strategies to protect against threats. They may use various tools and techniques to secure computer systems and networks, including firewalls, intrusion detection systems, encryption, and authentication protocols.

Some common techniques used in computer and network security include:

- *Firewalls:* Firewalls are software or hardware devices that monitor incoming and outgoing network traffic and block unauthorised access. They act as a barrier between the internal network and external networks, such as the internet.
- *Intrusion Detection Systems (IDS):* IDS are software or hardware devices that monitor network traffic for signs of suspicious or unauthorised activity. They can detect and alert security personnel to potential security threats.
- *Encryption:* Encryption converts data into a coded form to prevent unauthorised access. Those with the correct decryption key can only read encrypted data.
- *Authentication:* Authentication is the process of verifying a user's or device's identity. This can be achieved through the use of passwords, biometric identification, or smart cards.
- *Backup and Recovery:* Backup and recovery systems are used to create copies of critical data and applications to ensure they can be restored in the event of a security breach or system failure.

Computer and network security professionals must stay up-to-date with the latest security threats and technologies to protect against new and evolving threats. They may work in various industries, including government, finance, healthcare, and technology.

DATABASE MANAGEMENT SYSTEM

A Database Management System (DBMS) is a software application that helps users create, store, organise, and manage data. It provides an interface for users to interact with the database, allowing them to add, modify, delete, and retrieve data.

Some typical features of DBMS include:

Data security and access control: DBMS provides security measures to control access to data by authorised users only.

Data integrity: DBMS ensures the consistency and accuracy of data by enforcing constraints and validating data inputs.

Data backup and recovery: DBMS provides backup and recovery features to prevent data loss due to hardware or software failure.

Concurrent access and sharing: DBMS allows multiple users to access and modify data simultaneously, ensuring consistency and avoiding conflicts.

Query and reporting: DBMS provides tools to retrieve and analyse data from the database, allowing users to generate reports and gain insights.

Some examples of popular DBMS include Oracle, Microsoft SQL Server, MySQL, PostgreSQL, and MongoDB.

EMERGING TECHNOLOGIES

Emerging technologies refer to innovative technologies that are currently in the developmental stage and have the potential to revolutionise various industries. In computer science and engineering, emerging technologies are constantly being developed and adopted, and it is important for non-CSE students to have a basic understanding of them. Some examples of emerging technologies in computer science and engineering include:

Artificial intelligence (AI): AI involves the development of computer systems that can perform tasks that usually require human intelligence, such as speech recognition, decision-making, and problem-solving.

Machine learning (ML): ML is a subset of AI that involves the development of algorithms that can learn from data and improve over time.

Internet of Things (IoT): IoT involves connecting everyday objects to the Internet and enabling them to collect and share data.

Blockchain: Blockchain is a distributed, decentralised ledger technology that enables secure, tamper-proof transactions between parties without intermediaries like banks. It is essentially a digital ledger of transactions that are stored across a network of computers, with each block of data containing a unique cryptographic signature that links it to the previous block in the chain. One of the key benefits of blockchain is its ability to provide a high level of security and trust, as each transaction is verified and validated by a network of participants. Blockchain technology can transform many industries, from finance and banking to healthcare and supply chain management.

Augmented reality (AR) and virtual reality (VR): AR and VR technologies involve creating immersive, computer-generated environments that users can interact with.

Quantum computing: Quantum computing is an emerging field of computer science that uses quantum mechanics to process information. Unlike classical computers, which use binary bits (0s and 1s) to store and process information, quantum computers use quantum bits (qubits) that can exist in multiple states simultaneously. Quantum computing can solve complex problems beyond the capabilities of classical computers, such as optimising complex systems, simulating complex physical processes, and breaking encryption codes. However, quantum computing is still in its early stages, and practical applications are still being explored. One of the significant challenges with quantum computing is maintaining the stability of qubits, as they are susceptible to noise and interference. As a result, quantum computers are highly specialised and require shallow temperatures and other technical conditions to operate.

Metaverse: The metaverse is an emerging technology that refers to a collective virtual shared space created by the convergence of physical and virtual reality. It is often described as a fully immersive and interactive virtual world where people can interact with each other and digital objects in real time. The metaverse concept has been popularised in science fiction. However, it is now becoming a reality as advancements in virtual and augmented reality, blockchain, and other technologies enable the creation of immersive virtual worlds that can be accessed from anywhere. The potential applications of the metaverse are vast, including virtual events, social interactions, e-commerce, education, and more. However, there are also concerns about privacy, security, and the potential for addiction and social isolation. As the metaverse develops, it will likely become an increasingly important area of study and application for computer science and engineering.

These emerging technologies can transform various industries, including healthcare, finance, transportation, and more. Non-CSE students need to understand these technologies, their potential impact, and their ethical and social implications.

PRACTICE QUESTIONS

1. What is computer system engineering?
2. What are the main areas of focus in computer system engineering?
3. What are the hardware components of a computer system?
4. What are the software components of a computer system?
5. What is an operating system?
6. What are the primary functions of an operating system?
7. What is application software?
8. What are the typical features of a database management system?
9. What is distributed computing?
10. What is the Metaverse?

KEY TAKEAWAYS

- Computer system engineering involves designing, developing, testing, and evaluating computer systems, including hardware and software components.
- The main areas of focus in computer system engineering include computer hardware design and development, operating system design and optimisation, network design and optimisation, software engineering and development, embedded systems design and development, cybersecurity and information assurance, and human-computer interaction (HCI).
- Computer system engineers may work on various projects, including designing and developing computer hardware and software systems, implementing network infrastructure, and developing new technologies and applications.

- To be a successful computer system engineer, one must understand computer architecture, operating systems, programming languages, and other related technologies. In addition, they need to have strong problem-solving and critical thinking skills and the ability to work collaboratively with other engineers and stakeholders.

- The components of a computer system include the CPU, RAM, HDD/SSD, I/O devices, and GPU (hardware components) and the operating system, application software, system software, and programming software (software components).

- Operating systems and system software are critical components of computer systems, and they provide a platform for other software to run on. Application software is designed to help users perform specific tasks, and it differs from system software, which manages and controls computer hardware and other software programs.

- Distributed systems refer to a group of computers that work together as a single system to provide a standard set of services or functions. Networking is the process of connecting two or more computing devices to share resources and information.

- Database Management System (DBMS) is a software application that helps users create, store, organise, and manage data. It provides an interface for users to interact with the database, allowing them to add, modify, delete, and retrieve data.

- Emerging technologies in computer science and engineering include Artificial Intelligence (AI), Machine Learning (ML), Internet of Things (IoT), Blockchain, Augmented Reality (AR) and Virtual Reality (VR), Quantum Computing, and Metaverse. These technologies can transform various industries, including healthcare, finance, transportation, etc.

- Computer and network security is critical today, where cyber attacks are a significant threat. Operating systems provide features such as encryption, firewalls, and antivirus software to protect against various forms of attacks, including viruses, malware, and unauthorised access.

ANSWERS TO PRACTICE QUESTIONS

1. Computer system engineering involves designing, developing, testing, and evaluating computer systems, including hardware and software components, to optimise their performance and functionality while ensuring system security and reliability.

2. The main areas of focus in computer system engineering include computer hardware design and development, operating system design and optimisation, network design and optimiszation, software engineering and development, embedded systems design and development, cybersecurity and information assurance, and human-computer interaction (HCI).

3. The hardware components of a computer system include the CPU, RAM, hard disk drive or solid-state drive, input/output devices, and graphics processing unit (GPU).

4. The software components of a computer system include the operating system, application software, system software, and programming software.

5. An operating system is a software program that manages the computer's hardware and provides application services and interfaces.

6. The primary functions of an operating system include process management, memory management, file systems and storage management, and security and protection.

7. Application software is designed to help users perform specific tasks, such as word processing, spreadsheets, multimedia applications, and more.

8. The typical features of a database management system include data security and access control, data integrity, data backup and recovery, concurrent access and sharing, and query and reporting tools.

9. Distributed computing refers to a group of computers that work together as a single system to provide a standard set of services or functions, enabling sharing of resources, coordinating tasks, and managing data.

10. The metaverse is an emerging technology that refers to a collective virtual shared space created by the convergence of physical and virtual reality, often described as a fully immersive and interactive virtual world where people can interact with each other and digital objects in real time.

PROGRAMMING LANGUAGES

Programming languages are a fundamental aspect of computer science and engineering. They provide a set of rules and syntax that allow programmers to create instructions for a computer to follow.

Programming languages can be divided into several categories, including:

High-level programming languages: These languages are designed to be easily understood by humans and often use natural language-like syntax. Examples include Python, Java, C++, and JavaScript.

Low-level programming languages: These languages provide greater control over the hardware but are more difficult for humans to read and write. Examples include assembly language and machine code.

Scripting languages: These are specialised languages used to automate repetitive tasks and are often used in web development. Examples include PHP, Ruby, and Perl.

Functional programming languages: These are designed to handle mathematical computations and are often used in scientific and engineering applications. Examples include Haskell, Lisp, and ML.

Object-oriented programming languages: These languages are based on the concept of objects, which encapsulate data and the methods that operate on that data. Examples include Java, C++, and Python.

Domain-specific programming languages: These languages are designed for specific tasks or industries, such as SQL for database management or MATLAB for scientific computing.

Additionally, new and emerging programming languages are gaining popularity in the industry, such as Rust and Kotlin.

Understanding programming languages is essential for computer science and engineering students as they learn to create and develop software and applications.

OVERVIEW OF PROGRAMMING LANGUAGES

Programming languages are formal languages used to communicate with computers and other electronic devices. They are used to create software, scripts, and other applications that enable computers to perform tasks and automate processes. Programming languages can be categorised based on their abstraction, syntax, and functionality level.

Low-level programming languages, such as Assembly language and Machine language, provide a direct interface to computer hardware, allowing for precise control over system resources. These languages are often used to write operating systems, device drivers, and other software.

High-level programming languages, such as Python, Java, and C++, are designed to be more human-readable and easier to use, providing a more abstract programming layer for greater productivity and code reuse. These languages often come with extensive libraries and frameworks that can be used to build complex applications and systems.

Scripting languages, such as JavaScript, PHP, and Ruby, are designed to be lightweight and easy to use for quick prototyping and web development. They are often interpreted rather than compiled and used for creating dynamic web pages, server-side scripts, and other simple applications.

Domain-specific languages (DSLs) are specialised programming languages designed for specific tasks or industries, such as SQL for database management, MATLAB for scientific computing, and VHDL for hardware design.

Programming languages continue to evolve, and new languages are developed to address new challenges and opportunities. Emerging technologies, such as blockchain and artificial intelligence, are driving the development of new programming languages that can support these technologies.

IMPERATIVE PROGRAMMING LANGUAGES

Imperative programming languages are programming languages that allow the programmer to specify in a sequence of instructions how the problem is to be solved. Imperative programming languages focus on how the program is executed and how it changes the state of the computer. These languages are based on the Von Neumann architecture, which consists of a central processing unit (CPU), memory, and input/output (I/O) devices.

Examples of imperative programming languages include C, C++, Java, and Python. These languages are typically used for system programming, application programming, and scientific computing. They are designed to be efficient, low-level languages that can take full advantage of the hardware on which they run.

In an imperative programming language, the programmer specifies the sequence of steps the computer should take to solve a problem. This is typically done through statements or commands executed in order. The program is achieved by the CPU, which reads each statement and performs the action specified by the statement.

One advantage of imperative programming languages is that they are typically faster and more efficient than other programming languages. This is because they are designed to be executed directly by the CPU without an interpreter or other middleware. They are also easier to understand and debug since the program is executed in a linear sequence that is easy to follow.

However, one disadvantage of imperative programming languages is that they can be more difficult to write and maintain than other programming languages. The programmer must specify how the program will be executed, which can be complex and time-consuming. Additionally, these languages are less flexible than other programming languages since the program is tied to the specific hardware and architecture on which it is run.

OBJECT-ORIENTED PROGRAMMING LANGUAGES

Object-oriented programming languages use classes and objects to model real-world entities and their interactions. Object-oriented programming languages, such as Java, C++, and Python, are designed to support the object-oriented programming paradigm. This paradigm focuses on objects, which are instances of classes that encapsulate data and behaviour.

FUNCTIONAL PROGRAMMING LANGUAGES

Functional programming languages are a type of programming language based on functional programming principles. This programming paradigm focuses on creating software by composing functions and avoiding mutable and shared states.

The following features characterise functional programming languages:

Functions as First-Class Citizens: In functional programming languages, functions are treated as first-class citizens. They can be passed as arguments to other functions, returned as values from functions, and assigned to variables.

Immutable Data: Functional programming languages rely on immutable data, which means that once a value is created, it cannot be changed. This helps to eliminate bugs caused by unintentional changes to data.

Higher-Order Functions: Functional programming languages support higher-order functions, which are functions that take other functions as arguments or return functions as their results.

Recursion: Recursion is heavily used in functional programming languages to perform repetitive tasks.

Examples of functional programming languages include Haskell, Lisp, ML, F#, and Erlang. These languages are often used for scientific computing, data analysis, and distributed systems.

SCRIPTING LANGUAGES

Scripting languages are programming languages that are designed to automate the execution of tasks that would otherwise need to be performed manually. They are interpreted, which means that the code is executed without the need for compilation. Scripting languages are often used for tasks such as automating administrative tasks, data analysis, and web development.

Some popular scripting languages include:

Python: Python is a high-level, interpreted scripting language that is used for a wide range of applications, including web development, data analysis, machine learning, and artificial intelligence.

JavaScript: JavaScript is a scripting language primarily used for web development, such as creating interactive user interfaces and dynamic web applications.

Ruby: Ruby is a scripting language often used for web development, particularly with the Ruby on Rails framework. It is also used for other applications like data analysis and scripting.

PHP: PHP is a server-side scripting language primarily used for web development. It is often used in combination with web frameworks like Laravel or CodeIgniter.

Bash: Bash is a shell scripting language used primarily in Unix-based operating systems. It is often used for automating administrative tasks and system maintenance.

Scripting languages are generally easier to learn than compiled programming languages and are often combined with other programming languages. They are a powerful tool for automating tasks and increasing productivity.

MARKUP LANGUAGES

Markup languages are programming languages that format and style text-based documents, such as web pages and electronic documents. They are designed to add structure and meaning to text, allowing it to be interpreted and displayed consistently across different devices and platforms.

Some examples of markup languages include:

HTML (Hypertext Markup Language): The standard markup language for creating web pages. HTML uses various tags to describe a page's structure and content, including headings, paragraphs, links, and images.

XML (Extensible Markup Language): XML stores and transports data between different systems. It allows users to define their own tags and elements, making it highly flexible and customisable.

Markdown: Markdown is a lightweight markup language used to format text for the web and other digital media. It uses a simple syntax to denote headings, lists, links, and other formatting elements.

LaTeX: LaTeX is a markup language that is primarily used for typesetting scientific and mathematical documents. It allows users to define complex equations and mathematical notation using a simple syntax.

YAML (YAML Ain't Markup Language): YAML is a markup language that is used for data serialisation and configuration files. It is designed to be human-readable and easy to understand, making it a popular choice for developers and system administrators.

OBJECT-ORIENTED PROGRAMMING

Object-oriented programming (OOP) is a programming paradigm that is based on the concept of objects, which are instances of classes. In OOP, the focus is on the data and the operations that can be performed on that data, rather than on the algorithms that are used to manipulate that data.

The main features of object-oriented programming include:

Encapsulation: Encapsulation refers to the idea of bundling data and the methods that operate on that data into a single unit, called a class. This enables data to be hidden from other parts of the program, and ensures that it can only be accessed through the methods provided by the class.

Inheritance: Inheritance is a class's ability to inherit another class's properties and methods. This enables the creation of hierarchies of classes, with the more general classes at the top and the more specific classes at the bottom.

Polymorphism: Polymorphism refers to the ability of different objects to be treated as the same type of object. This enables the creation of code that can work with various objects, without needing to know the details of each object's implementation.

Object-oriented programming languages include Java, C++, Python, Ruby, and many others. Object-oriented programming has become widespread in software development due to its ability to manage complexity and improve code reusability.

OBJECT-ORIENTED PROGRAMMING CONCEPTS

Object-oriented programming (OOP) is a programming paradigm based on the concept of objects, which can contain data and code to manipulate that data. The following are some key concepts in OOP:

Objects: Objects are instances of classes defined by a blueprint specifying the objects' attributes and methods.

Classes: A class is a template for creating objects. It defines the properties and methods that an object can have.

Inheritance: Inheritance is a mechanism that allows a new class to be based on an existing class. The new class inherits the properties and methods of the existing class.

Encapsulation: Encapsulation is the practice of hiding the implementation details of a class from the outside world. This is achieved by defining the properties and methods of the class as either public, private, or protected.

Polymorphism: Polymorphism is the ability of objects of different classes to be treated as objects of the same class. This is achieved through method overloading and method overriding.

Abstraction: Abstraction is the process of representing complex real-world objects in a simplified manner. It involves focusing on the essential features of an object and ignoring the non-essential ones.

These concepts are fundamental to OOP and are used to create modular, reusable, and easy-to-maintain complex software systems.

CLASSES AND OBJECTS

In object-oriented programming (OOP), a class is a blueprint or template for creating objects, which are instances of the class. A class defines a set of properties and methods that are common to all instances of that class.

Objects are instances of a class and represent specific instances of the properties and methods defined in the class. Each object has its own set of values for the properties defined in the class, and can invoke the methods of the class.

For example, a class representing a car would define properties such as the car's make, model, and colour and methods such as starting the engine and turning on the headlights. An object of the car class would represent a specific car with a particular make, model, and colour, and could invoke the methods of the class to start the engine or turn on the headlights.

In object-oriented programming, objects interact with one another through methods and messages. When an object sends a message to another object, it invokes a method on that object. The method then performs some action or computation and returns a result or updates the state of the object.

Classes and objects are fundamental concepts in OOP and are used extensively in software development to create reusable and modular code.

For example, let's say we want to create a program to model a bank account. We could define a " BankAccount " class containing data and methods relevant to bank accounts. Here's an example in Python:

Python

```
class BankAccount:
    def __init__(self, account_number, balance):
        self.account_number = account_number
        self.balance = balance
```

```
def deposit(self, amount):
    self.balance += amount

def withdraw(self, amount):
    if self.balance >= amount:
        self.balance -= amount
    else:
        print("Insufficient funds")

def get_balance(self):
    return self.balance
```

In this example, the *'BankAccount'* class has two data attributes: *'account_number'* and *'balance'*. It also has three methods: *'deposit'*, *'withdraw'*, and *'get_balance'*. The *'__init__'* method is a special method called a constructor that is used to initialise the object's attributes when it is created.

To create an object of the *'BankAccount'* class, we can call the class constructor and pass in the required parameters:

Makefile

```
account1 = BankAccount("123456789", 1000)
```

Now we have an object named *'account1'* of the *'BankAccount'* class with an *'account_number'* of "123456789" and a *'balance'* of 1000. We can call its methods to perform operations on the account:

scss

```
account1.deposit(500)
account1.withdraw(200)
print(account1.get_balance())
```

This will output *'1300'*, as we deposited 500 and withdrew 200 from the initial balance of 1000.

In summary, classes and objects provide a powerful way to organise and structure code in object-oriented programming, allowing for efficient and modular development of complex systems.

INHERITANCE AND POLYMORPHISM

Inheritance and polymorphism are two fundamental concepts in object-oriented programming (OOP).

Inheritance refers to the ability of a class to inherit properties and methods from a parent class, known as the base or superclass. The class that inherits the properties and methods is called the derived or child class. Inheritance enables code reusability and promotes modular design, as common code can be defined in a parent class and reused in multiple derived classes. For example, if there is a class called "Vehicle" that has common properties and methods like "number of wheels," "color," and "start engine," then a child class "Car" can inherit these properties and methods from "Vehicle" and add its own properties and methods specific to cars.

Polymorphism refers to the ability of objects of different classes to be treated as if they were of the same class. In other words, it allows objects of different classes to be used interchangeably. This is achieved through inheritance and method overriding. For example, in the vehicle hierarchy, both "Car" and "Motorcycle" can inherit from the "Vehicle" class and define their own implementations of the "start engine" method. The client code can then call the "start engine" method on a "Vehicle" object, and the correct implementation will be called based on the actual type of the object at runtime.

Inheritance and polymorphism are essential concepts in OOP that enable code reusability, modularity, and flexibility in designing complex software systems.

In the example below, we have a parent class *'Animal'* that has a method *'makeSound()'*. We also have two child classes *'Dog'* and *'Cat'* that extend the *'Animal'* class and override the *'makeSound()'* method with their own implementation.

In the main class, we create an instance of the *'Animal'* class and call the *'makeSound()'* method, which outputs "The animal makes a sound". We also create instances of the Dog and Cat classes and assign them to Animal references. When we call the makeSound() method on these instances, the output is different based on the implementation in their respective child classes. This demonstrates the concept of polymorphism, where objects of different types can be treated as objects of a common parent class and behave differently based on their individual implementations.

---

java

```java
// Parent class
class Animal {
  public void makeSound() {
    System.out.println("The animal makes a sound");
  }
}

// Child class that extends the Animal class
class Dog extends Animal {
  @Override
  public void makeSound() {
    System.out.println("The dog barks");
  }
}

// Child class that extends the Animal class
class Cat extends Animal {
  @Override
  public void makeSound() {
    System.out.println("The cat meows");
  }
}

// Main class
class Main {
  public static void main(String[] args) {
    Animal animal = new Animal(); // Create an instance of the Animal class
```

---

animal.makeSound(); // Output: The animal makes a sound

Animal dog = new Dog(); // Create an instance of the Dog class and assign it to an Animal reference
dog.makeSound(); // Output: The dog barks

Animal cat = new Cat(); // Create an instance of the Cat class and assign it to an Animal reference
cat.makeSound(); // Output: The cat meows
}
}

ENCAPSULATION AND ABSTRACTION

Encapsulation and abstraction are two important concepts in object-oriented programming that help to achieve data hiding, modularity, and code reusability.

Encapsulation is wrapping data and code into a single unit, called a class, and hiding the implementation details from the user. This means that the user can access only the public methods and properties of the class, while the private methods and properties remain hidden. Encapsulation provides a high degree of security and helps prevent unauthorised data access.

Abstraction is the process of hiding the implementation details of a class and exposing only the essential features to the user. In other words, abstraction simplifies complex systems by breaking them into smaller, more manageable parts. Abstraction helps to reduce complexity, increase reusability, and make code more modular.

Encapsulation and abstraction help create more robust, secure, and maintainable code.

COMMON OBJECT-ORIENTED PROGRAMMING LANGUAGES

Here are some common object-oriented programming languages and their details:

Java: Java is a popular object-oriented programming language first released in 1995. Java is known for its robustness, security, and scalability. It is platform-independent, meaning it can run on any operating system, and is widely used for building web applications, mobile apps, and desktop applications.

Python: Python is a high-level, interpreted programming language often used for data science, machine learning, and web development. It is known for its simplicity and readability and has a large and active community of developers contributing to its development and maintenance.

C#: C# (pronounced "C sharp") is a modern, object-oriented programming language developed by Microsoft. It is designed for building Windows desktop applications, web applications, and games and is often used in conjunction with the .NET framework.

Ruby: Ruby is a dynamic, object-oriented programming language that is often used for web development and scripting. It is known for its simplicity and expressiveness and has a large and active community of developers contributing to its development and maintenance.

Swift: Swift is a powerful, open-source programming language developed by Apple for building iOS, macOS, watchOS, and tvOS applications. It is designed to be easy to learn and use and is known for its safety, speed, and performance.

PHP: PHP is a server-side scripting language that is often used for web development. It is known for its simplicity and ease of use and is widely used for building dynamic websites and web applications.

JavaScript: JavaScript is a popular scripting language that is used for web development and client-side scripting. It is known for its versatility and can be used for various applications, including web and mobile app development, game development, and more.

Kotlin: Kotlin is a modern, statically typed programming language that is designed to be interoperable with Java. It is often used for Android app development and is known for its concise syntax and ease of use.

These are just a few examples of common object-oriented programming languages. Each language has its own unique features and benefits, and the choice of language often depends on the specific needs and requirements of a project.

KEY TAKEAWAYS

Key takeaways from the "Object-Oriented Programming" section:

- Object-oriented programming (OOP) is based on the concept of objects, which are instances of classes.
- OOP focuses on data and operations that can be performed on that data rather than algorithms.
- Encapsulation, inheritance, and polymorphism are key features of OOP.
- Encapsulation refers to bundling data and methods into a class to hide data from other program parts.
- Inheritance allows a new class to inherit properties and methods from existing classes, promoting code reusability.
- Polymorphism allows objects of different classes to be treated as the same object type.
- Classes and objects are fundamental concepts in OOP and are used to create modular, reusable, and easy-to-maintain complex software systems.

Key takeaways from the "Classes and Objects" section:

- A class is a blueprint for creating objects with common properties and methods.
- Objects are instances of a class and represent specific instances of the properties and methods defined in the class.
- Objects interact with one another through methods and messages.
- Software development uses classes and objects to create reusable and modular code.

Key takeaways from the "Inheritance and Polymorphism" section:

- Inheritance allows a new class to inherit properties and methods from existing classes, promoting code reusability.
- Polymorphism allows objects of different classes to be treated as the same object type.
- Inheritance and polymorphism enable code reusability, modularity, and flexibility in designing complex software systems.

Key takeaways from the "Encapsulation and Abstraction" section:

- Encapsulation is wrapping data and code into a single unit, called a class, and hiding the implementation details from the user.
- Abstraction is the process of hiding the implementation details of a class and exposing only the essential features to the user.
- Encapsulation and abstraction help create more robust, secure, and maintainable code.

Key takeaways from the "Common Object-Oriented Programming Languages" section:

- Java, Python, C#, Ruby, Swift, PHP, JavaScript, and Kotlin are all common object-oriented programming languages.

- Each language has its own unique features and benefits, and the choice of language often depends on the specific needs and requirements of a project.

PRACTICE QUESTIONS AND ANSWERS

Object-Oriented Programming:

1. What is object-oriented programming based on?
   - Answer: Object-oriented programming is based on the concept of objects, which are instances of classes.
2. What is encapsulation in object-oriented programming?
   - Answer: Encapsulation refers to the bundling of data and the methods that operate on that data into a single unit, called a class.
3. What is polymorphism in object-oriented programming?
   - Answer: Polymorphism refers to the ability of different objects to be treated as the same type of object.
4. What are some object-oriented programming languages?
   - Answer: Some object-oriented programming languages include Java, C++, Python, and Ruby.
5. Why has object-oriented programming become widespread in software development?
   - Answer: Object-oriented programming has become widespread in software development due to its ability to manage complexity and improve code reusability.

Classes and Objects:

1. What is a class in object-oriented programming?
   a. Answer: A class is a blueprint or template for creating objects, which are instances of the class.
2. What is an object in object-oriented programming?

    a.   Answer: An object is an instance of a class and represents specific instances of the properties and methods defined in the class.

3.   What is the purpose of a constructor in a class?

    a.   Answer: A constructor is a special method called when an object of a class is created. It is used to initialize the object's attributes.

4.   What is the difference between a class and an object?

    a.   Answer: A class is a blueprint for creating objects, while an object is an instance of a class.

5.   What is the purpose of methods in a class?

    a.   Answer: Methods in a class are used to define the class's behaviour and enable the manipulation of the class's data.

Inheritance and Polymorphism:

1.   What is inheritance in object-oriented programming?

    a.   Answer: Inheritance is a mechanism that allows a new class to be based on an existing class, inheriting its properties and methods.

2.   What is a superclass in object-oriented programming?

    a.   Answer: A superclass is a parent class from which another class is derived.

3.   What is polymorphism in object-oriented programming?

    a.   Answer: Polymorphism refers to the ability of objects of different classes to be treated as if they were of the same class.

4.   What is method overriding in object-oriented programming?

    a.   Answer: Method overriding is a technique in which a child class provides a different implementation of a method that is already defined in its parent class.

5. What is the purpose of inheritance and polymorphism in object-oriented programming?
    a. Answer: Inheritance and polymorphism enable code reusability, modularity, and flexibility in designing complex software systems.

Encapsulation and Abstraction:

1. What is encapsulation in object-oriented programming?
    a. Answer: Encapsulation refers to the practice of hiding the implementation details of a class from the outside world, defining the properties and methods of the class as public, private, or protected.
2. What is an abstraction in object-oriented programming?
    a. Answer: Abstraction is the process of simplifying complex real-world objects, focusing on an object's essential features and ignoring the non-essential ones.
3. What is the difference between encapsulation and abstraction?
    a. Answer: Encapsulation is about hiding the implementation details of a class, while abstraction is about simplifying complex systems by breaking them into smaller, more manageable parts.
4. What are some benefits of encapsulation and abstraction in object-oriented programming?
    a. Answer: Encapsulation and abstraction help create more robust, secure, and maintainable code.
5. How do encapsulation and abstraction help achieve code reusability?
    a) Answer: Encapsulation and abstraction enable the creation of modular, reusable, and easy-to-maintain complex software

SOFTWARE DESIGN PROCESS

Software design defines a software system's architecture, components, modules, interfaces, and data. It is the process of transforming user requirements into an implementation specification.

The software design process defines a software system's architecture, components, modules, interfaces, and data. It is an iterative process that involves the following steps:

Requirements gathering and analysis: This is the first step in the software design process. It involves gathering and analysing the requirements of the software system. Requirements gathering involves talking to stakeholders and end-users to understand their needs and requirements. Requirements analysis involves breaking down the requirements into smaller, more manageable pieces.

Specification and design: In this step, the software design team creates a detailed specification and design document. This document describes the software architecture, components, modules, interfaces, and data.

Implementation and coding: The software design team implements the design document by writing code in this step. The code is written in a programming language that is appropriate for the software system.

Testing: Once the software system has been implemented, it is tested to ensure that it meets the requirements. Testing involves running the software system and checking that it behaves as expected.

Maintenance: Once the software system is in use, it may need to be updated or modified to meet changing requirements. This is known as maintenance. Maintenance involves fixing bugs, adding new features, and improving the software system's performance.

The software design process is integral to the software development life cycle. A well-designed software system is easier to maintain, extend, and more reliable.

DESIGN PRINCIPLES

Design principles are guidelines or recommendations software developers and designers use to create effective and efficient software systems. These principles are based on best practices and have been established through experience and research. They help software designers and developers create scalable, maintainable, and extensible software. Some of the commonly used design principles are:

SOLID Principles

SOLID stands for Single Responsibility Principle, Open/Closed Principle, Liskov Substitution Principle, Interface Segregation Principle, and Dependency Inversion Principle. They aim to make software systems more modular, flexible, and easier to maintain. Robert C. Martin introduced these principles in his book "Agile Software Development: Principles, Patterns, and Practices".

KISS Principle

KISS stands for Keep It Simple, Stupid. The KISS principle states that software systems should be kept as simple as possible. This means that unnecessary complexity should be avoided and the design should be as straightforward to understand as possible.

DRY Principle

DRY stands for Don't Repeat Yourself. The DRY principle states that software developers should avoid repeating code and functionality in multiple places. This can be achieved by using modular design, code re-use, and inheritance.

YAGNI Principle

YAGNI stands for You Ain't Gonna Need It. The YAGNI principle states that software developers should avoid adding functionality that is not necessary at the current time. This means that software systems should be designed to meet current needs and that future requirements should be addressed when they arise.

GRASP Principles

GRASP stands for General Responsibility Assignment Software Patterns. The GRASP principles are guidelines for assigning responsibilities to objects in object-oriented software design. They aim to promote the design of software systems that are easy to understand, maintain, and extend.

Composition Over Inheritance Principle

The Composition Over Inheritance principle suggests that software developers should prefer composition over inheritance when designing software systems. This means that objects should be composed of other objects instead of inheriting functionality from parent classes.

Law of Demeter Principle

The Law of Demeter, also known as the Principle of Least Knowledge, states that objects should have limited knowledge of other objects. This means that objects should only interact with objects directly related to them, not with objects indirectly related.

Single Responsibility Principle

The Single Responsibility Principle states that each class or module should have only one responsibility. This means that classes and modules should be designed to do one thing and do it well, and that they should not be responsible for multiple tasks.

Open/Closed Principle

The Open/Closed Principle states that software systems should be designed to be open for extension but closed for modification. This means the design should allow new functionality to be added without modifying existing code.

Interface Segregation Principle

The Interface Segregation Principle states that interfaces should be designed to be as small and specific as possible. This means interfaces should only include the methods necessary for the objects that implement them.

Design principles are guidelines that software developers and designers use to create effective and efficient software systems. These principles aim to promote modularity, flexibility, maintainability, and extensibility. By following these principles, software designers and developers can create software systems that are easier to understand, maintain, and extend.

DESIGN PATTERNS

Design patterns have been used in software development for many years and are now considered a fundamental part of software engineering. Design patterns are reusable solutions to commonly occurring problems in software design. They provide a standardised way of solving problems that can be adapted to different situations.

There are three main categories of design patterns:

Creational Patterns

Creational patterns are used to create objects and classes to promote flexibility and reuse. These patterns deal with object creation mechanisms, trying to create objects in a manner suitable to the situation.

Examples of creational patterns include:

- *Singleton pattern:* This pattern ensures that a class has only one instance and provides a global access point to that instance.
- *Factory pattern:* This pattern provides an interface for creating objects but allows subclasses to alter the type of objects that will be created.
- *Abstract Factory pattern:* This pattern provides an interface for creating families of related or dependent objects without specifying their concrete classes.

Structural Patterns

Structural patterns define the relationships between objects and classes to form larger, more complex structures. These patterns deal with object composition, making creating complex things from simpler ones possible.

Examples of structural patterns include:

- *Adapter pattern:* This pattern converts the interface of a class into another interface that clients expect. It allows classes with incompatible interfaces to work together.
- *Facade pattern:* This pattern provides a unified interface to a set of interfaces in a subsystem. It simplifies the interaction between the client and the subsystem.
- *Decorator pattern:* This pattern adds behaviour to an individual object, either statically or dynamically, without affecting the behaviour of other objects.

Behavioural Patterns

Behavioural patterns manage algorithms, relationships, and responsibilities between objects and classes. These patterns deal with communication between objects and delegating responsibilities between them.

Examples of behavioural patterns include:

Observer pattern: This pattern defines a one-to-many dependency between objects so that all its dependents are notified and updated automatically when one object changes state.

Strategy pattern: This pattern defines a family of algorithms, encapsulates each one, and makes them interchangeable. It allows the algorithm to vary independently from clients that use it.

Template method pattern: This pattern defines the skeleton of an algorithm in a method, deferring some steps to subclasses. It allows subclasses to redefine certain steps of an algorithm without changing the algorithm's structure.

Design patterns help to improve the design and architecture of software systems by providing proven solutions to common problems. By using design patterns, developers can create more flexible, extensible, and maintainable software.

DESIGN TOOLS

Design tools are software applications designers use to create and present their work. They help designers to create and communicate their ideas effectively. Some popular design tools include:

Sketch: Sketch is a vector graphics editor designed specifically for web and UI design. It features a simple and intuitive interface that makes creating wireframes, prototypes, and designs easy.

Adobe Creative Suite: The Adobe Creative Suite is a collection of design tools that includes Photoshop, Illustrator, InDesign, and others. These tools are widely used in graphic, web, and other design fields.

Figma: A web-based design tool that allows teams to collaborate in real time on design projects. It features a powerful vector editing tool, prototyping capabilities, and design systems.

InVision: InVision is a design collaboration, prototyping, and feedback platform. It allows designers to create interactive prototypes, share them with stakeholders, and collect feedback.

Canva: Canva is a graphic design tool that allows users to create various designs, from social media graphics to business cards and presentations. It features an intuitive drag-and-drop interface and a vast library of templates and design elements.

Axure RP: Axure RP is a wireframing and prototyping tool that allows designers to create interactive prototypes and documentation for web and mobile applications. It features a drag-and-drop interface and a wide range of design elements.

SketchUp: SketchUp is a 3D modelling tool for architectural, interior, and landscape architecture design. It features a user-friendly interface and a wide range of tools for creating and editing 3D models.

These are just a few examples of design tools available for designers. Each tool has its unique features and benefits, and the choice of tool often depends on the specific needs and requirements of the project.

DESIGN TRADE-OFFS

In the software design process, trade-offs must be made between different design options or goals. Here are some common design trade-offs:

Functionality vs Performance: A software system may have various features and functionalities, but adding more features can negatively impact performance. Designers must find a balance between providing the desired functionality and maintaining an acceptable level of performance.

Maintainability vs Complexity: A software system that is easy to maintain is usually simple, but a simple design may not meet all the requirements. Designers must balance the system's complexity and maintainability to ensure that it is both effective and easy to maintain.

Flexibility vs Specificity: A flexible design allows for future changes and adaptations, but a design that is too flexible may be less efficient or less specific to the current needs. Designers must determine the optimal level of flexibility while still meeting the system's specific requirements.

Cost vs Quality: A higher-quality software system often requires more resources and cost. Designers must balance the cost of development and the level of quality needed for the system to meet its goals.

Usability vs Security: A software system that is easy to use may not always be secure, and a security system may not always be easy to use. Designers must balance the system's usability and security to ensure the user can easily use the system while protecting sensitive data.

Innovation vs Compatibility: An innovative design may not be compatible with existing technologies or systems, making integrating challenging. Designers must balance the system's level of innovation with its compatibility with existing technologies.

Understanding these trade-offs is essential for making informed decisions during the software design process. By balancing competing design goals, designers can create a software system that meets users' needs while also being efficient, effective, and maintainable.

DESIGN DOCUMENTATION

Design documentation is a crucial aspect of the software design process, as it helps ensure that the software system meets the requirements and is developed in a maintainable and extensible way. Effective design documentation provides a clear and detailed description of the software system's architecture, components, modules, interfaces, and data and the design decisions made during the software design process.

Some of the reasons why documentation is important in the software design process are:

Ensures clarity: Design documentation ensures the design is clear and easily understandable to everyone involved in the development process, including developers, testers, and stakeholders.

Facilitates maintenance: Design documentation helps developers to maintain the software system more efficiently by providing a roadmap of the software's architecture and design.

Provides a reference: Design documentation serves as a reference for future development efforts, helping developers to avoid repeating mistakes and to reuse code and design elements.

Helps with communication: Design documentation facilitates communication between team members, as well as with stakeholders and clients, ensuring that everyone is on the same page and has a shared understanding of the software system.

Enables scalability: Design documentation helps to ensure that the software system can be easily scaled and extended as new requirements arise.

To create effective design documentation, some guidelines that can be followed include:

Be clear and concise: Design documentation should be clear and concise, avoiding technical jargon and focusing on the key aspects of the design.

Use visual aids: Visual aids such as diagrams, flowcharts, and tables can help to make the design documentation more accessible and easier to understand.

Include relevant details: Design documentation should include all relevant details of the design, including the software system's architecture, components, modules, interfaces, and data.

Be organised: Design documentation should be collected logically and consistently, with clear headings and subheadings.

Be up-to-date: Design documentation should be kept up-to-date as the software system evolves, ensuring that it accurately reflects the software's architecture and design.

There are different types of design documentation, including design specifications, design documents, and design reviews. Design specifications are high-level documents that outline the software system's architecture, components, and interfaces. Design documents are more detailed documents that describe the software system's design and implementation, including code samples and detailed specifications. Design reviews are meetings where stakeholders and team members review and discuss the design documentation.

Overall, adequate design documentation is critical to the success of the software design process, providing a roadmap for the development of a maintainable, extensible, and reliable software system.

DESIGN DOCUMENT TEMPLATE

The design Document should include the following:

- Project Name:
- Version:
- Date:
- Table of Contents

  - Introduction
  - Requirements
  - System Architecture
  - Data Design
  - Interface Design
  - Component Design
  - Security Design
  - Performance Design
  - Testing
  - Maintenance
  - Glossary

Introduction
This section provides an overview of the software design and its purpose.

Requirements
This section lists the requirements of the software system and how they are addressed in the design.

System Architecture
This section describes the system architecture, including the overall structure and the components that make up the system.

Data Design

This section describes the data design, including the database schema and how the data will be stored, accessed, and manipulated.

Interface Design

This section describes the user interface design, including the user interface components, how they will be used, and how they will be integrated into the system.

Component Design

This section describes the component design, including the design of individual software components and how they will interact with each other.

Security Design

This section describes the security design, including how the system will protect against unauthorised access, how data will be secured, and how security will be integrated into the system design.

Performance Design

This section describes the performance design, including how the system will handle high volumes of data and users and ensure it performs optimally under different conditions.

Testing

This section describes the testing strategy and plan, including how the software system will be tested and the expected outcomes of each test.

Maintenance

This section describes the maintenance plan, including how updates and modifications will be managed and how issues and bugs will be addressed.

Glossary

This section includes a glossary of terms used in the design document.

Appendix A: Technical Specifications

This section includes technical specifications for the hardware and software components of the system.

Appendix B: Use Cases

This section includes use cases for the software system, including user interactions and expected outcomes.

Appendix C: Class Diagrams

This section includes class diagrams that depict the relationships and interactions between the software system's classes.

Appendix D: Sequence Diagrams

This section includes sequence diagrams that depict the interactions between different parts of the software system.

Appendix E: Flow Charts

This section includes flow charts that depict the logic and flow of different parts of the software system.

Appendix F: User Manual

This section includes a user manual that provides instructions on using the software system.

Note: The above sections and appendices are just examples, and a design document template may vary based on the project and the needs of the stakeholders.

KEY TAKEAWAYS

Understanding User Requirements:
- Gather user requirements through direct communication or analysis of user behaviour and feedback.
- Prioritise requirements and logically organise them to facilitate design decisions.

Software Design Principles:
- Follow design principles such as SOLID and DRY to ensure a modular and scalable design.
- Use abstraction, encapsulation, and inheritance to improve the design's maintainability and flexibility.
- Consider factors such as performance, security, and usability in the design process.

Design Patterns:
- Design patterns provide reusable solutions to common design problems.
- Understand and apply design patterns such as Creational, Structural, and Behavioral patterns.
- Use design patterns to create a flexible and scalable software design.

Testing and Validation:
- Automated testing frameworks such as ServiceNow ATF validate and test the software design.
- Create functional, performance, and integration tests to ensure the software meets the user requirements and quality standards.
- Use email notifications or other forms of reporting to communicate the test results to the relevant stakeholders.

PRACTICE QUESTIONS AND ANSWERS

1. What is the purpose of following design principles such as SOLID and DRY in software design?
   - Answer: The purpose of following design principles such as SOLID and DRY is to create a modular and scalable software design that is easy to maintain and extend over time.
2. What is the importance of understanding user requirements in software design?
   - Answer: Understanding user requirements is essential in software design because it helps create a design that meets the users' needs, leading to better user adoption and satisfaction.
3. What are some factors to consider when designing software for performance?
   - Answer: Factors to consider when designing performance software include efficient algorithms, proper data structures, and appropriate caching techniques.
4. What is the purpose of design patterns in software design?
   - Answer: The purpose of design patterns in software design is to provide reusable solutions to common design problems, leading to better code quality and maintainability.
5. What is the difference between abstraction and encapsulation in software design?
   - Answer: Abstraction is the process of reducing complexity by hiding unnecessary details, while encapsulation is the process of bundling data and methods together into a single unit to prevent external interference.
6. How can automated testing frameworks such as ServiceNow ATF help in software design?
   - Answer: Automated testing frameworks such as ServiceNow ATF can help in software design by allowing developers to

validate the software design against user requirements and quality standards in an automated and efficient manner.

7. What are some benefits of following modular design principles in software design?
   - Answer: Benefits of following modular design principles in software design include better code organisation, increased code reusability, and improved maintainability.
8. How can design patterns create a flexible and scalable software design?
   - Answer: Design patterns can create a flexible and scalable software design by providing reusable solutions to common design problems, improving code quality and maintainability.
9. What are some best practices for designing software with security in mind?
   - Answer: Best practices for designing software with security in mind include validating user input, using encryption techniques, implementing access controls, and keeping software up-to-date with security patches.
10. How can user feedback be used to improve the software design process?
    - Answer: User feedback can be used to improve the software design process by identifying areas of the design that are not meeting user requirements or are causing user frustration, leading to better user adoption and satisfaction over time.

INTRODUCTION TO PROGRAMMING

INTRODUCTION TO PROGRAMMING

Programming is creating computer programs, which are instructions that tell a computer what to do. Programs are written in programming languages like Java, Python, C++, and many others.

Programming is used to create various software applications, from web applications to mobile apps, games, and more. Programming can also be used to automate tasks, such as data processing or system administration, and control devices, like robots or sensors.

The primary goal of programming is to create software applications that can automate tasks, solve problems, or enhance the capabilities of existing systems. Programming is used in various fields, including web development, mobile app development, game development, data analysis, and scientific research.

To become proficient in programming, one needs to learn the basic concepts and techniques of programming, such as data types, control structures, functions, and object-oriented programming. It is also important to learn how to use integrated development environments (IDEs), software tools that programmers use to write, test, and debug their code.

Programming requires patience, attention to detail, and problem-solving skills. It's a dynamic field that requires continuous learning and adaptation to new technologies and programming languages.

Learning to program can be challenging, but many resources are available to help beginners get started. Online courses, coding boot camps, and programming communities can provide valuable guidance and support to those interested in programming.

PROGRAMMING CONCEPTS AND PRINCIPLES

Programming concepts and principles are the foundation of writing computer programs. By learning these concepts and practising with examples, non-CSE students can gain the skills to build their programs.

Here are some of the programming concepts and principles that are commonly taught to beginners:

Variables: A variable is like a container that holds a value. It has a name, and you can store different things, like numbers, words, or true/false statements. For example, you might have a variable called "age" with the value 25.

Data types: Different kinds of things you can store in variables are called "data types." Examples include numbers (like 5 or 3.14), words (like "hello" or "world"), and true/false statements (like "yes" or "no"). Understanding data types is important because you need to know what kind of data you're working with to do the right things.

Control structures: Control structures help you control what your program does. For example, if/else statements let you make decisions based on whether something is true or false. Loops let you repeat a piece of code multiple times. For example, you might use a loop to add up all the numbers in a list.

Loops: Loops let you do something repeatedly until you're done. There are different types of loops, but they all work similarly: you set a condition for when the loop should stop, and the loop keeps going until that condition is met. For example, you might use a loop to print out all the numbers from 1 to 10.

Functions: Functions are like little programs inside your program. They take some inputs (like variables), do some work, and then give you some outputs (like a value or a message). For example, you might have a " add " function that takes two numbers as inputs and returns their sum.

Scope: Scope is like a set of rules for variables and functions in your program. Understanding scope is important because you need to know what variables and functions are available in different parts of your program. For example, if you define a variable inside a function, it might not be available outside that function.

Arrays and lists: Arrays and lists let you store multiple values in one variable. For example, you might have a list of numbers that you want to add up. Instead of creating a separate variable for each number, you can put them all in a list and then use a loop to add them up.

Strings: Strings are like words or phrases in your program. They're made up of a bunch of characters, like letters and numbers. Understanding strings is important because you'll often work with text in your programs. For example, you might use a string to store someone's name or to print out a message on the screen.

GRAPHICAL USER INTERFACE (GUI) PROGRAMMING

Graphical user interface (GUI) programming is a type of programming that involves creating user interfaces for software applications. A user interface allows users to interact with an application, and a GUI is a type of user interface that uses graphical elements such as buttons, text boxes, and menus.

GUI programming involves using a programming language to create the visual components of an application and the code that governs how those components behave. Here are some common graphical elements that can be used in GUI programming:

Buttons: Buttons are graphical elements that users can click on to perform an action, such as submitting a form or closing a window.

Text boxes: Text boxes allow users to input text, such as their name or email address.

Labels: Labels display text or other information, such as a window's title or a button's name.

Menus: Menus allow users to choose from a list of options, such as a list of file types or a list of settings.

Checkboxes and radio buttons: Checkboxes and radio buttons allow users to select one or more options from a list.

Sliders: Sliders allow users to select a value within a range, such as a volume control or a brightness setting.

GUI programming involves creating these graphical elements and then writing the code governing their behaviour. For example, when a user clicks a button, the code might trigger a specific action or function.

Many programming languages, including Java, C#, Python, and JavaScript, can be used for GUI programming. Each language has its tools and libraries for creating GUI applications.

GUI programming is essential for building modern software applications with user-friendly interfaces. Programmers can create interactive and engaging user applications by learning to create graphical elements and write the code that governs their behaviour.

ERROR HANDLING

Error handling is dealing with problems that can occur in a computer program. These problems are called "errors" or "bugs," and they can happen for many reasons, such as incorrect input, faulty code, or unexpected system behaviour. Error handling is important because it helps prevent programs from crashing or producing incorrect results.

Here are some common strategies for handling errors in a program:

Validation: Validation is the process of checking input data to make sure it meets certain criteria. For example, if a program asks for a user's age, it might validate that the input is a number between 0 and 150. This helps prevent errors caused by invalid input.

Exception handling: Exception handling is a way of dealing with errors during program execution. When an error occurs, the program can "throw" an exception, a message describing the error. The program can then "catch" the exception and take appropriate action, such as displaying an error message or retrying the operation.

Logging: Logging is the process of recording events or actions in a program. This can be helpful for debugging errors or understanding how a program is behaving. For example, a program might log errors to a file or database so developers can review them later.

Defensive programming: Defensive programming is a way of writing code that anticipates and handles errors. This involves using techniques like checking input data, validating assumptions, and adding error-handling code. Defensive programming helps create more robust and reliable programs.

For example, imagine you are building a program that takes a user's age and calculates the cost of a movie ticket. If the user enters a negative age, the program might throw an exception and display an error message. The program might also log the error to a file for debugging purposes.

For example, imagine you are building a program that reads data from a file. If the file does not exist or cannot be read, the program might throw an exception and display an error message. The program might also retry the operation or log the error for debugging purposes.

Error handling is integral to programming because it helps create more reliable and easier-to-use programs. By learning how to handle errors effectively, non-technical students can become better programmers and create more robust software applications.

DEBUGGING

Debugging is the process of finding and fixing errors, or bugs, in a program. When a program doesn't work as expected, debugging can help identify and correct the problem's source.

Here are some common strategies for debugging a program:

Print statements: One of the simplest ways to debug a program is to add print statements to show the value of variables or the flow of execution. For example, suppose a program is supposed to calculate the sum of two numbers but the output is incorrect. In that case, you might add print statements to show the values of the variables used in the calculation.

Step-by-step execution: Many programming environments have tools that allow you to step through a program one line at a time. This can help you understand how the program executes and identify where errors occur.

Breakpoints: Breakpoints are specific places in a program where you can pause execution and examine the program's state. This can help you identify errors that occur at specific points in the program.

Logging: Logging can be helpful for debugging errors that occur in a deployed program. By logging events or actions in the program, you can better understand how the program is behaving and identify errors that occur in the real world.

For example, imagine you are building a program that calculates the average grade of a group of students. If the program produces incorrect output, you might add print statements to show the values of the variables used in the calculation. You might also use step-by-step execution to see how the program executes and identify where the error occurs. If the error is hard to identify, you might add a breakpoint to pause execution at a specific point and examine the program's state.

In another example, imagine you are building a program that reads data from a file. If the program crashes when it tries to read the file, you might add print statements to show the program's state at the time of the error. You might also use logging to record the error and understand how it occurs in the real world.

MODULAR PROGRAMMING

Modular programming is the practice of breaking a program down into smaller, more manageable pieces. Each piece of the program, called a module or function, is responsible for a specific task or set of tasks. By breaking a program down into modules, programmers can create easier code to write, test, and maintain.

Here are some benefits of modular programming:

Reusability: When code is broken down into modules, it can be reused in different parts of the program or different programs altogether. This can save time and effort in development and make it easier to maintain code over time.

Scalability: As a program grows larger, it can become more difficult to manage and maintain. Breaking a program down into smaller modules makes it easier to scale up or down as needed.

Debugging: As we saw earlier, when errors occur in a program, it can be easier to identify and fix them when the code is modular. This is because each module is responsible for a specific task or set of tasks, making it easier to locate errors and fix them quickly.

Collaboration: When multiple programmers work on a program, modular programming can help make it easier for them to work together. Each programmer can work on a different module, making it easier to divide the work and ensure the code is consistent and well-organized.

For example, imagine you are building a program that calculates the meal cost at a restaurant. Instead of writing all the code in one large program, you might break the code down into modules, such as a module for calculating the meal cost, a module for calculating the tax, and a module for calculating the tip. Each module is responsible for a specific task and can be reused in other parts of the program or in other programs altogether.

In another example, imagine you are building a program that reads data from a database and displays it on a web page. Instead of writing all the code in one large program, you might break the code down into modules, such as a module for connecting to the database, a module for retrieving data, and a module for displaying data on the web page. Each module is responsible for a specific task and can be reused in other parts of the program or in other programs altogether.

ALGORITHM DESIGN

Algorithm design is the process of creating step-by-step procedures, called algorithms, for solving a problem or accomplishing a task. Algorithms are an essential part of programming, and understanding how to design and implement them is important for creating effective and efficient software applications.

Here are some common steps involved in algorithm design:

Identify the problem: The first step in algorithm design is to identify the problem you're trying to solve. This could be anything from calculating the average of a list of numbers to sorting a list of names alphabetically.

Break the problem down into smaller parts: Once you've identified the problem, you need to break it down into smaller, more manageable parts. This can help you focus on one aspect of the problem at a time and create more efficient algorithms.

Determine the steps needed to solve each part: For each part of the problem, you need to determine the steps needed to solve it. These steps should be simple and easy to understand.

Combine the steps into a complete algorithm: Once you've determined the steps needed to solve each part of the problem, you can combine them into a complete algorithm. The algorithm should be easy to follow and should solve the problem efficiently.

Here are some examples of algorithms:

Finding the maximum number in a list: To find the maximum number in a list, you could start by setting a variable to the first number in the list. Then, you could loop through the rest of the list, comparing each number to the variable and updating it if the number is larger. At the end of the loop, the variable should contain the maximum number in the list.

Sorting a list of names: To sort a list of names alphabetically, you could start by comparing the first two names in the list. You could swap their positions if the first name comes before the second name alphabetically. Then, you could compare the second and third names in the list, and so on, until the entire list is sorted.

DATA ANALYSIS

Data analysis is the process of using programming to manipulate and analyse data. This involves using tools and libraries, such as Pandas and NumPy, to read data, clean it, and perform various operations on it.

Here are some common techniques used in data analysis:

Reading in data: Data can be stored in various formats, such as CSV files or Excel spreadsheets. To read data, you need to use a library that can handle the format you're working with.

Cleaning data: Data often comes with errors or inconsistencies, such as missing values or incorrect data types. To clean data, you need to identify and correct these errors.

Transforming data: Data can be transformed in various ways, such as converting text to lowercase or scaling numeric values between 0 and 1. These transformations can help make the data more useful for analysis.

Analysing data: Once the data is cleaned and transformed, you can perform various analyses on it, such as calculating summary statistics or creating visualisations.

Here are some examples of data analysis tasks:

Finding the mean and standard deviation of a set of numbers: To find the mean and standard deviation of a set of numbers using Python, you could use the NumPy library. NumPy provides functions like "mean" and "std" that can be used to calculate these statistics.

Cleaning a dataset: To clean a dataset using Python, you could use the Pandas library. Pandas provide functions for handling missing values, correcting data types, and removing duplicates.

Creating a visualisation: To create a visualisation of data using Python, you could use a library like Matplotlib or Seaborn. These libraries provide functions for creating various types of plots, such as scatterplots or histograms.

KEY TAKEAWAYS

- Programming involves creating instructions for a computer to follow.
- Programming languages are used to write these instructions.
- The software development process involves several stages: planning, design, coding, testing, and maintenance.
- Programming concepts and principles include variables, data types, control structures, loops, functions, scope, arrays and lists, and strings.
- Graphical user interface (GUI) programming involves creating interactive programs with buttons, text boxes, menus, and other graphical elements.
- Error handling is anticipating, detecting, and resolving errors or issues in a program.
- Debugging is the process of finding and fixing errors in a program.
- Modular programming involves breaking a program down into smaller, more manageable pieces.
- Algorithm design involves creating step-by-step procedures, called algorithms, for solving a problem or accomplishing a task.
- Data analysis involves using programming to manipulate and analyze data using libraries such as Pandas and NumPy.
- Programming can be used in various industries like finance, healthcare, and gaming.
- Learning programming can improve problem-solving skills and enhance career opportunities.
- Many resources are available for learning programming, including online courses, books, and tutorials.
- Collaboration and communication are important skills for programming teams.
- Good code involves writing clear, concise, and maintainable code.

PRACTICE QUESTIONS AND ANSWERS

1. What is programming?
    i. Answer: Programming involves creating instructions for a computer to follow.
2. What are programming languages used for?
    i. Answer: Programming languages are used to write these instructions.
3. What are the stages of the software development process?
    i. Answer: The software development process involves several stages, including planning, design, coding, testing, and maintenance.
4. What are some programming concepts and principles?
    i. Answer: Programming concepts and principles include variables, data types, control structures, loops, functions, scope, arrays and lists, and strings.
5. What is GUI programming?
    i. Answer: GUI programming involves creating interactive programs with buttons, text boxes, menus, and other graphical elements.
6. What is error handling?
    i. Answer: Error handling is the process of anticipating, detecting, and resolving errors or issues in a program.
7. What is debugging?
    i. Answer: Debugging is the process of finding and fixing errors in a program.
8. What is modular programming?
    i. Answer: Modular programming involves breaking a program down into smaller, more manageable pieces.
9. What is algorithm design?

      i. Answer: Algorithm design involves creating step-by-step procedures, called algorithms, for solving a problem or accomplishing a task.

10. What is data analysis in programming?

      i. Answer: Data analysis involves using programming to manipulate and analyze data using libraries such as Pandas and NumPy.

PROJECTS WITH HELP

Here are some very simple projects with help for you to practice.

Calculator: Create a simple calculator that can add, subtract, multiply, and divide two numbers. This project can be resolved by using basic programming concepts such as variables, control structures, and functions. You can use a programming language such as Python or JavaScript to create the calculator.

Guess the number game: Create a game where the computer picks a random number, and the user has to guess it. You can create the game using a programming language such as Java or C++. This project can be resolved by using basic programming concepts such as variables, control structures, and user input/output.

Tic Tac Toe game: Create a simple Tic Tac Toe game that two players can play. You can use a programming language such as Python or JavaScript to create the game. This project can be resolved by using basic programming concepts such as variables, control structures, and user input/output.

Text editor: Create a simple text editor that allows users to create, edit, and save text files. You can use a programming language like Java or C# to create the text editor. This project can be resolved by using basic programming concepts such as user input/output, file handling, and control structures.

Password generator: Create a simple password generator that generates random passwords based on user preferences such as length and complexity. You can use a programming language such as Python or JavaScript to create the password generator. This project can be resolved using basic programming concepts such as variables, control structures, and user input/output.

These projects are relatively simple and can be a good starting point for non-technical students new to programming. They can also be expanded upon and made more complex as the students gain more experience and knowledge.

CODING A PROJECT

Here is an example code for a simple password generator in Python:

Python

```python
import random
import string

def generate_password(length, uppercase, lowercase, digits, special_chars):
    # Define character sets to use for password
    uppercase_chars = string.ascii_uppercase if uppercase else ''
    lowercase_chars = string.ascii_lowercase if lowercase else ''
    digit_chars = string.digits if digits else ''
    special_chars = string.punctuation if special_chars else ''

    # Combine character sets based on user preferences
    password_chars = uppercase_chars + lowercase_chars + digit_chars + special_chars

    # Generate password by randomly selecting characters from character set
    password = ''.join(random.choice(password_chars) for i in range(length))

    return password

# Example usage
password = generate_password(10, True, True, True, False)
```

```
print(password)
```

In this code, the **'generate_password'** function takes five arguments: **'length'** (length of the password), uppercase (whether to include uppercase letters in the password), **'lowercase'** (whether to include lowercase letters in the password), digits (whether to include **'digits'** in the password), and **'special_chars'** (whether to include special characters in the password).

The function first defines the character sets to use for the password based on user preferences. It then combines this character sets into a single **'password_chars'** string. Finally, it generates the password by randomly selecting characters from the **'password_chars'** string and concatenating them together.

In the example usage, the function is called with arguments to generate a 10-character password with uppercase letters, lowercase letters, and digits, but no special characters. The resulting password is then printed to the console.

TESTING THE CODE

You can run the code directly from the Python interpreter or by running a Python file with the .py extension.

To test the password generator code, you can do the following:

1. Open a text editor and copy the code into a new file. Save the file with a .py extension (e.g. password_generator.py).
2. Open a terminal or command prompt and navigate to the directory where you saved the password_generator.py file.
3. Run the following command to execute the script:

```
python password_generator.py
```

This will run the script and print the generated password to the console.

Alternatively, you can try the code online using a website such as Repl.it or Online Python Compiler. Here are the steps to do this on Repl.it:

1. Go to https://repl.it/ and create a new Python project.
2. Copy the password generator code into the main Python file (usually called main.py).
3. Click on the "Run" button to execute the code.
4. In the console window, you should see the generated password printed out.

Online compilers may have some limitations compared to running the code locally on your computer.

WEB DEVELOPMENT

Web development refers to the creation and maintenance of websites and web applications. It involves a combination of technical and creative skills to design, develop, and deploy web-based software products.

The web development process typically involves several stages, including:

Planning: This involves defining the objectives of the website or web application, identifying the target audience, and creating a plan to achieve the desired goals.

Design: This involves creating the visual and functional aspects of the website or web application, including the user interface, navigation, and layout.

Development: This involves the actual coding of the website or web application, including the use of programming languages such as HTML, CSS, JavaScript and server-side programming languages such as PHP, Ruby, Python, or .NET.

Testing: This involves testing the website or web application for functionality, performance, and usability, as well as identifying and fixing any bugs or errors.

Deployment: This involves deploying the website or web application to a live server or web hosting service, making it available for public use.

Web development can range from simple static websites to complex web applications that require databases, APIs, and user authentication. Some common types of web applications include content management systems (CMS), e-commerce websites, social media platforms, and online booking systems.

Web development also involves knowledge of web standards and best practices, including search engine optimisation (SEO), web accessibility, and responsive design. With the increasing popularity of mobile devices, web developers also need to ensure that websites and web applications are optimised for mobile devices and different screen sizes.

TECHNICAL SKILLS REQUIRED

1. HTML: The markup language used to structure content on web pages.
2. CSS: Cascading Style Sheets used to style the HTML content and layout of web pages.
3. JavaScript: A programming language used to add interactivity, functionality, and animations to web pages.
4. Server-side scripting languages: such as PHP, Python, Ruby, or Node.js, are used to generate dynamic content on the server side and interact with databases.

5. Relational databases: such as MySQL, PostgreSQL, or Oracle, are used to store and manage website data.

6. Web servers: such as Apache or Nginx, are used to host and deliver web content to users.

7. Version control, like Git, is used to track changes and manage collaboration among team members.

8. APIs: Application Programming Interfaces enabling communication between systems and software applications.

9. Web development frameworks and libraries such as React, Angular, Vue.js, or jQuery provide pre-built components and functionality to speed up web development.

10. Responsive design: the ability to design and build optimised websites for viewing on different devices and screen sizes.

11. Performance optimisation: optimising web page loading times, reducing file sizes, and improving server response times.

12. Testing and debugging: using tools like Chrome Developer Tools or Firebug to diagnose and fix errors in web pages and scripts.

HOW TO OBTAIN THE TECHNICAL SKILLS

1. HTML/CSS: W3Schools (https://www.w3schools.com/html/default.asp)

2. JavaScript: Codecademy (https://www.codecademy.com/learn/introduction-to-javascript)

3. Backend languages (e.g. Python, Ruby, PHP): Udemy (https://www.udemy.com/topic/python-web-development/)

4. Frontend frameworks (e.g. React, Angular, Vue.js): React (https://reactjs.org/), Angular (https://angular.io/), Vue.js (https://vuejs.org/)

5. Mobile app development: Android (https://developer.android.com/training/basics/firstapp), iOS (https://developer.apple.com/library/archive/referencelibrary/GettingStarted/DevelopiOSAppsSwift/)

6. Database management: MySQL (https://www.mysql.com/), MongoDB (https://www.mongodb.com/)
7. APIs: Postman (https://www.postman.com/)
8. Git: GitHub (https://github.com/)
9. Testing: Cypress (https://www.cypress.io/), Jest (https://jestjs.io/)
10. DevOps: Docker (https://www.docker.com/), Kubernetes (https://kubernetes.io/)
11. Cloud computing: Amazon Web Services (https://aws.amazon.com/), Microsoft Azure (https://azure.microsoft.com/), Google Cloud Platform (https://cloud.google.com/)
12. Security: OWASP (https://owasp.org/)

SOFT SKILLS REQUIRED FOR WEB DEVELOPMENT

In addition to technical skills, web developers also need strong, soft skills to succeed. Here are some soft skills that non-CSE students should focus on when learning web development:

Communication: Good communication skills are essential in any field, particularly web development. Web developers must communicate effectively with clients, project managers, and other team members to ensure everyone is on the same page.

Teamwork: Web development is rarely a solo effort. Web developers need to work effectively as part of a team, collaborating with other developers, designers, and project managers.

Problem-solving: Web development can be challenging and requires a lot of problem-solving. Non-CSE students learning web development must be comfortable working through complex issues and finding creative solutions.

Attention to detail: Web development requires much attention to detail. A single error in the code can cause the entire website to break. Non-CSE students learning web development need to be meticulous and detail-oriented.

Time management: Web development projects often have tight deadlines, and non-CSE students need to manage their time effectively to meet those deadlines.

Adaptability: Web development is constantly evolving, and non-CSE students need to adapt to new technologies, languages, and tools as they become available.

Creativity: Web development is also an art form, and non-CSE students need to be able to think creatively to come up with engaging and visually appealing websites.

APP DEVELOPMENT

App development refers to creating software applications that run on mobile devices such as smartphones and tablets. These applications are designed to provide users with specific functionalities, such as accessing social media, playing games, or managing personal finances.

App development can be divided into two main categories: native and hybrid. Native apps are built specifically for a single platform, such as iOS or Android, and are written in the programming language that is native to that platform, such as Swift for iOS and Java or Kotlin for Android. On the other hand, hybrid apps are built using web technologies like HTML, CSS, and JavaScript and can be run on multiple platforms using frameworks like Apache Cordova or React Native.

The app development process involves several stages: conceptualisation, design, development, testing, and deployment. Here's a brief overview of each stage:

Conceptualisation: This stage involves identifying the problem that the app will solve and defining its purpose and features. This includes conducting market research, creating user personas, and developing a user flow.

Design: In this stage, the app's user interface and user experience are designed. This includes creating wireframes, prototypes, and visual designs.

Development: This is where the actual coding of the app takes place. The features that were defined in the conceptualization stage are implemented in the chosen programming language, following best practices and guidelines for the specific platform.

Testing: Once the app has been developed, it is tested to ensure that it is functional, user-friendly, and bug-free. Testing can include manual testing, automated testing, and user testing.

Deployment: After the app has been thoroughly tested, it is released to the app store for users to download and use.

Examples of apps include social media platforms like Facebook and Twitter, gaming apps like Angry Birds and Candy Crush, e-commerce apps like Amazon and eBay, and productivity apps like Evernote and Google Drive. App development is a constantly evolving field, with new technologies and trends always emerging, and it requires a combination of technical skills and creative problem-solving abilities.

SOFTWARE IN APP DEVELOPMENT

Many software tools are available for app development, and the choice often depends on the type of app being developed and the target platform. Here are some examples:

Android Studio: This is the official IDE (Integrated Development Environment) for Android app development. It is an all-in-one tool that includes a code editor, a visual layout editor, a debugger, and a suite of tools for testing and deploying apps.

Xcode: This is the official IDE for iOS app development. It includes a code editor, a graphical user interface editor, a debugger, and a simulator for testing apps on different devices and operating systems.

React Native: This is an open-source framework for building cross-platform mobile apps. It allows developers to write code in JavaScript and use a single codebase to develop apps for both iOS and Android.

Xamarin: This cross-platform app development framework allows developers to write code in C# and use a single codebase to develop iOS, Android, and Windows apps.

Flutter: This is a relatively new open-source mobile app development framework created by Google. It allows developers to build high-performance, native apps for iOS and Android using a single codebase written in the Dart programming language.

PhoneGap: This is an open-source framework for building cross-platform mobile apps using web technologies such as HTML, CSS, and JavaScript. It allows developers to build apps that run on iOS, Android, and Windows devices.

Adobe XD: This is a design tool that allows designers to create user interfaces and interactive prototypes for mobile apps. It has built-in tools for creating wireframes, visual designs, and animations.

These are just a few examples of the many software tools available for app development. The choice of tool often depends on the developer's skillset, the type of app being developed, and the target platform.

APP DEVELOPMENT LANGUAGES

Several programming languages can be used for app development. The choice of language depends on the specific requirements of the app, the target platform, and the developer's familiarity with the language.

Here are some commonly used programming languages for app development:

Java: Java is a popular object-oriented programming language used for developing Android apps. It is one of the most widely used languages in the world and has a large community of developers. Many Android development tools are written in Java, making them a good choice for developing Android apps.

Swift: Swift is a relatively new programming language that Apple created for iOS, iPadOS, macOS, watchOS, and tvOS development. It is a modern, powerful, and easy-to-learn language that works well with Apple's Cocoa and Cocoa Touch frameworks.

Kotlin: Kotlin is a cross-platform programming language used to develop Android, iOS, and web apps. Kotlin is gaining popularity as an alternative to Java for Android development. It was developed by JetBrains, the same company that created the popular IntelliJ IDEA IDE.

C#: C# is a modern, object-oriented programming language developed by Microsoft. It is used for developing Windows, Android, and iOS apps. C# is a popular language for creating games for Xbox and Windows platforms.

JavaScript: JavaScript is a popular programming language used for web development, but it can also be used for developing mobile apps using frameworks like React Native and Ionic. It is a versatile language that can be used for both front-end and back-end development.

Objective-C: Objective-C is an object-oriented programming language used to develop iOS and macOS apps. It was the primary language used for iOS development before the introduction of Swift.

Python: Python is a popular programming language that can be used for various applications, including web development, data analysis, and machine learning. It can also be used for developing mobile apps using frameworks like Kivy and BeeWare.

These are just a few programming languages that can be used for app development. The choice of language depends on several factors, including the target platform, the features required, and the developer's experience and familiarity with the language.

WAYS TO BUILD A MOBILE APP WITH NO TECH SKILLS

There are several ways to build a mobile app with no tech skills. Here are some options:

Use an app builder platform: Several app builder platforms are available that allow you to create mobile apps without coding or programming skills. These platforms provide pre-built templates, drag-and-drop interfaces, and other tools to create an app quickly and easily. Some examples of these platforms include Appy Pie, BuildFire, and AppMakr.

Hire a freelancer or app development company: If you have a budget, you can hire a freelancer or app development company to create an app. You can find freelancers and companies on Upwork, Freelancer, or Fiverr. Be sure to check their portfolios and reviews before hiring them.

Use WordPress plugins: If you have a WordPress website, you can use plugins such as AppPresser or WP-AppKit to turn your website into a mobile app.

Use online app makers: Online app makers such as Glide, Thunkable, and Bubble allow you to create mobile apps without coding. These platforms provide drag-and-drop interfaces and pre-built templates.

Use templates: To design your app, you can use pre-built templates available on platforms such as Sketch, Figma, or Adobe XD. You can hire a developer or use an app builder platform to turn your design into a functional app.

LOW-CODE, NO-CODE FOR APP DEVELOPMENT

Low-code and no-code platforms refer to software development platforms that allow users to create applications using visual interfaces and configuration options instead of writing code manually. These platforms simplify software development and enable non-technical users to build applications without programming skills.

In a low-code platform, developers can use a visual interface to drag and drop pre-built components to create an application. This process involves minimal coding, and the platform handles the underlying infrastructure and backend code. In contrast, a no-code platform provides pre-built templates and components that users can customize without writing any code.

Low-code and no-code platforms have become increasingly popular because they enable businesses to develop applications more quickly and cost-effectively than traditional software development approaches. They can also help bridge the gap between business needs and IT resources, as business users can develop their own applications without extensive IT support.

Examples of low-code and no-code platforms include Microsoft PowerApps, Google App Maker, Zoho Creator, and Salesforce Lightning. These platforms provide users with pre-built templates, drag-and-drop interfaces, and configuration options that enable them to create custom applications quickly and easily.

DEVELOP APPS WITHOUT TECHNICAL KNOWLEDGE

Several platforms allow non-technical users to create and develop mobile apps without knowing how to code. Here are some examples:

Appy Pie: This popular no-code app development platform lets users build apps for iOS, Android, and other platforms. It offers a drag-and-drop interface, pre-built templates, and various features like push notifications, in-app purchases, and social media integration.

Bubble: Bubble is a visual programming platform that enables users to create web and mobile applications without coding. It offers a drag-and-drop interface and a range of customization options to create fully functional apps.

Glide: Glide is a no-code platform that lets users create mobile apps directly from Google Sheets. Users can add data to a Google Sheet, and the app will be automatically generated with features like forms, user profiles, and messaging.

Adalo: Adalo is a no-code platform that allows users to create native mobile apps for iOS and Android. It offers a drag-and-drop interface, pre-built components, and integrations with various third-party tools.

AppSheet: AppSheet is a no-code platform that allows users to create mobile and web apps from spreadsheets and data sources. It offers a range of features like mapping, image recognition, and chatbots.

These platforms are designed to simplify the app development process and make it accessible to anyone, regardless of technical skills. They offer a range of customization options and pre-built templates, so users can create fully functional apps without writing any code.

INDEX

- Agile Methodology: An iterative and incremental approach to software development that emphasises flexibility, collaboration, and customer satisfaction.
- BIOS (Basic Input/Output System): Firmware used to initialise and test hardware components during the boot process of a computer.
- Central Processing Unit (CPU) - The CPU is the "brain" of the computer that performs calculations and controls the flow of information.
- CLI: A Command-Line Interface (CLI) is a user interface requiring users to enter text commands to interact with a computer system—Graphical User Interface (GUI) vs. Command-Line Interface (CLI).
- Cloud Computing: Cloud computing is delivering computing services, such as servers, storage, databases, and software, over the internet. It allows users to access these services on-demand without needing on-site infrastructure.
- Code Editors: Software applications designed specifically for editing and writing code, providing features such as syntax highlighting, code completion, and code navigation.

- Computer Hardware: Computer hardware refers to the physical components of a computer, such as a motherboard, CPU, RAM, storage devices, and input/output devices.
- Computer Networks: A computer network is a collection of computers and other devices that are connected together to share resources and communicate with each other.
- Computer System: A computer system is a combination of hardware and software that works together to perform computing tasks.
- CPU: The Central Processing Unit (CPU) is the computer's brain that performs most of the processing of instructions.
- Debuggers: Software tools used by developers to identify and fix errors, defects, and other issues in software systems.
- DNS (Domain Name System): A system that translates domain names (such as www.google.com) into IP addresses that computers can use to communicate over a network.
- Edge Computing: Edge computing is a distributed computing paradigm that brings computation and data storage closer to the location where it is needed to improve response time and save bandwidth.
- Ethernet is a wired networking technology that uses cables to connect devices to a network.
- Ethernet Port: An Ethernet port is a connector on a computer that is used to connect to a wired network. Its function is to send and receive data between the computer and other devices on the network.
- File System - A method operating systems use to organise and store files and directories on a storage device.
- FPGA (Field-Programmable Gate Array): An integrated circuit that can be programmed and reprogrammed after manufacturing to perform specific logic functions.
- FTP (File Transfer Protocol): A protocol used for transferring files between computers over a network.

- Graphical User Interface (GUI) - An interface that allows users to interact with a computer using graphical elements, such as icons and menus.
- GUI: A Graphical User Interface (GUI) is a user interface that allows users to interact with a computer system using visual elements such as icons, buttons, and menus.
- Hard Disk Drive (HDD) - A type of storage device that uses spinning disks to store and retrieve data.
- HCI (Human-Computer Interaction): The study of how humans interact with computers and how to design computer systems that are easy to use and intuitive for humans.
- History of Software Engineering: An overview of the evolution of software engineering as a discipline from its early beginnings to modern software development practices.
- Integrated Development Environment (IDE): A software application that provides comprehensive tools and features for developing software, including code editors, debuggers, compilers, and build tools.
- Interaction: Interaction refers to how users interact with a computer system, including the user interface, input devices, and output devices.
- Introduction to Software Engineering: A discipline concerned with the systematic approach to software development, operation, and maintenance.
- IoT (Internet of Things): A network of interconnected devices that are able to collect and exchange data through the internet.
- IP (Internet Protocol): A protocol used for routing data packets between devices on a network, including the internet.
- IP Address - A unique identifier assigned to each device on a network, allowing them to communicate with each other using the Internet Protocol.

- Kanban Methodology: A visual workflow management approach that emphasizes continuous delivery and improvement, flexibility, and collaboration.
- Lean Methodology: A management philosophy and approach to software development that focuses on minimising waste, optimising resources, and maximising value for the customer.
- Local Area Network (LAN) - A network that covers a small area, such as a home, office, or school.
- Motherboard - The motherboard is the main circuit board in a computer that connects all the components together.
- NTFS (New Technology File System): A file system used by modern versions of the Windows operating system that provides advanced features such as file compression, encryption, and permissions.
- Operating System (OS) - The software that manages the computer hardware and software resources and provides common services for computer programs.
- PaaS (Platform as a Service): A cloud computing service model in which a provider offers a platform for users to develop, run, and manage applications.
- Protocol: A protocol is a set of rules and standards that dictate how devices on a network communicate with each other.
- Random Access Memory (RAM) - RAM is a volatile memory that temporarily stores data that the CPU is currently working on.
- Read-Only Memory (ROM) - ROM is a type of non-volatile memory that stores data that cannot be modified.
- ROM: Read-Only Memory (ROM) is a type of non-volatile memory that stores data that cannot be modified.
- Router - A networking device connecting multiple networks and directing data traffic between them.
- SaaS (Software as a Service): A cloud computing service model in which a provider offers access to software applications hosted on their servers and accessed over the internet.

- Scrum Methodology: A framework for agile software development that emphasises teamwork, communication, and iterative progress towards a well-defined goal.
- Serverless Computing - A model of cloud computing where the cloud provider manages the infrastructure and automatically allocates resources as needed.
- SMTP (Simple Mail Transfer Protocol): A protocol for sending email messages between computers over a network.
- Software Configuration Management: The process of identifying, organising, and controlling changes to software products and related artifacts throughout the software development life cycle.
- Software Design: The process of creating a detailed plan or blueprint for a software system that defines its architecture, components, interfaces, and data.
- Software Development Life Cycle (SDLC): The process of developing software, from the initial planning stage through maintenance and support.
- Software Development Methodologies: The various approaches to developing software systems, each with its own set of principles, practices, ahd techniques.
- Software Development Tools: The various software tools used by software developers to design, code, test, debug, and maintain software systems.
- Software Maintenance: The process of modifying, updating, or otherwise changing existing software to correct errors, improve performance, or enhance functionality.
- Software Metrics and Measurement: The process of quantifying and evaluating various aspects of software products, processes, and resources to improve software quality, productivity, and efficiency.
- Software Project Management: The discipline of planning, organising, and managing resources to successfully complete

software projects on time, within budget, and to specified quality standards.

- Software Quality Assurance (SQA): The process of ensuring that software products and processes meet the specified requirements and quality standards.
- Software Requirements: The process of identifying, analysing, documenting, and validating the needs and constraints of stakeholders for a software system.
- Software Testing: The process of evaluating a software system or component to determine whether it meets the specified requirements and quality standards.
- Solid-State Drive (SSD) - A type of storage device that uses flash memory to store and retrieve data.
- TCP (Transmission Control Protocol): A protocol used for transmitting data over a network in a reliable and ordered manner.
- Testing Frameworks: Software tools and libraries used by developers to automate and manage software testing processes and tasks.
- TLS (Transport Layer Security): A security protocol that provides secure communication over a network, often used for secure web browsing and email.
- UDP (User Datagram Protocol): A protocol used for transmitting data over a network in a fast and unreliable manner.
- UEFI (Unified Extensible Firmware Interface): A newer type of firmware used to initialize and test hardware components during the boot process of a computer, replacing the older BIOS system.
- Usability: Usability is the degree to which specified users can use a system to achieve specified goals with effectiveness, efficiency, and satisfaction in a specified context.
- UX (User Experience): The overall experience that a user has when interacting with a computer system or application, encompassing factors such as ease of use, efficiency, and satisfaction.

- Version Control Systems (VCS): Software tools and practices for managing changes to source code and other software artefacts, enabling collaboration and version control.
- Virtualisation: Virtualisation is creating a virtual version of a computing resource, such as a server, operating system, or network. It is used to run multiple virtual machines on a single physical machine.
- VPN (Virtual Private Network): A network connection that provides a secure, private connection over a public network such as the internet.
- WAN (Wide Area Network): A network of connected devices that are located in a large geographic area, such as a country or the entire world.
- Waterfall Methodology: A linear, sequential approach to software development that divides the development process into distinct phases, each of which must be completed before proceeding to the next.

LIST OF ABBREVIATIONS

Abbreviation	Full Form
AI	Artificial Intelligence
ALU	Arithmetic Logic Unit
API	Application Programming Interface
AR	Augmented Reality
AWS	Amazon Web Services
BIOS	Basic Input/Output System
CFS	Common File System
CLI	Command-Line Interface
CMS	Content Management System
CPU	Central Processing Unit
CRUD	Create
CSS	Cascading Style Sheets
CU	Control Unit
DNS	Domain Name System
DNS	Domain Name System
FAT32	File Allocation Table 32-bit
FPGA	Field-Programmable Gate Array
FTP	File Transfer Protocol
FTP	File Transfer Protocol
GCP	Google Cloud Platform
GUI	Graphical User Interface
HCI	Human-Computer Interaction
HDD	Hard Disk Drive
HTML	Hypertext Markup Language

Abbreviation	Full Form
HTTP	Hypertext Transfer Protocol
I/O	Input/Output
IaaS	Infrastructure as a Service
ICT	Information and Communication Technology
IDE	Integrated Development Environment
IoT	Internet of Things
IP	Internet Protocol
JS	JavaScript
JSON	JavaScript Object Notation
LAN	Local Area Network
NT	New Technology
NTFS	New Technology File System
ORM	Object Relational Mapping
PaaS	Platform as a Service
PC	Personal Computer
RAM	Random Access Memory
REST	Representational State Transfer
ROM	Read-Only Memory
SaaS	Software as a Service
SDK	Software Development Kit
SMTP	Simple Mail Transfer Protocol
SQL	Structured Query Language
SSD	Solid-State Drive
SSH	Secure Shell
SSL	Secure Sockets Layer
TCP	Transmission Control Protocol
TLS	Transport Layer Security

Abbreviation	Full Form
UDP	User Datagram Protocol
UEFI	Unified Extensible Firmware Interface
UI	User Interface
URL	Uniform Resource Locator
UX	User Experience
VCS	Version Control System
VPN	Virtual Private Network
VR	Virtual Reality
XML	Extensible Markup Language

TABLE OF FIGURES

OTHER BOOKS IN THIS SERIES

This book is part of a series of books written on Computer Science Engineering (CSE) for the non-CSE Enthusiasts' initiative by Enamul Haque.

Book – 1	*Book – 2*	*Book – 3*
Introduction to Computer Systems and Software Engineering	Introduction to Mathematics for Computing (Algorithms and Data Structures)	Introduction to Digital literacy and the future of computing

ISBN:	ISBN:	ISBN:
9781447790563	9781447771302	9781445273921

Available: at https://www.lulu.com/spotlight/authorenam

ABOUT THE AUTHOR

Enamul Haque (এনামুল হক) is an industry veteran and thought leader with almost 30 years of experience in the IT industry. Over the course of his career, Enamul has worked with some of the world's most reputable companies, including Wipro, Microsoft, Capgemini, Nokia, and HCL Technologies, as well as international organisations like the United Nations High Commissioner for Refugees (UNHCR) and International Telecommunication Union (ITU).

As a data whisperer, Enamul is renowned for his expertise in AI-driven RPA (Intelligent Process Automation), service integration and management, and digital transformation. He has helped several Fortune 500 businesses navigate the rapidly changing technology landscape and capitalise on its opportunities.

Enamul is also an accomplished author and researcher with many writing topics, including IT Service Management, Cloud Computing, AI, IoT, and Big Data analytics. His deep understanding of the industry and ability to stay at the forefront of technological advancements have made him a sought-after speaker and guest lecturer at the University of Coventry's London campus.

Enamul holds a licence en science Informatique from the University of Geneva, a degree in mathematics and analytics from the Swiss Federal Institute of Technology (EPFL), Lausanne, and a degree in machine learning and AI from the University of Helsinki. He recently received a leadership and mentoring certification from Harvard Business School.

Enamul's vast and diverse experience, combined with his passion for technology and its impact on the world, makes him a true thought leader in the industry. He stays at the forefront of emerging trends and is dedicated to helping organisations embrace digital transformation and thrive in today's ever-evolving technology landscape.

Enamul has been at the forefront of some of the most significant technological advancements of the past three decades, including the rise of cloud computing, artificial intelligence, and the internet of things. Throughout his career, he has consistently demonstrated his ability to anticipate trends and identify opportunities for innovation. Enamul's expertise in service integration and management has been precious in helping organisations navigate the complex landscape of emerging technologies and ensure they stay ahead of the curve. His passion for lifelong learning has kept him on the cutting edge of IT innovation, and he is always excited to share his insights with others.

In addition to his work in the IT industry, Enamul is an accomplished author and researcher. He has published numerous articles on topics ranging from IT service management to cloud computing to big data analytics. He is a sought-after speaker and has presented at conferences and seminars worldwide. Enamul's ability to explain complex technical concepts in accessible language has made him a valuable resource for businesses looking to stay up-to-date with the latest developments in the IT field.

Enamul is also committed to giving back to his community. Whether mentoring young professionals, volunteering with local charities, or leading tech initiatives in developing countries, Enamul is dedicated to making a difference in the world. He has volunteered with several non-profit organisations over the years and is passionate about using technology to impact society positively. He believes that the IT industry is responsible for promoting social good, and he always looks for ways to use his expertise to help those in need.

Get all my books from here: https://www.lulu.com/spotlight/authorenam

NOTES AND REFERENCES

[i] Photo by Andrea Piacquadio: https://www.pexels.com/photo/man-in-white-crew-neck-t-shirt-holding-laptop-3799837/

[2] Abacus explained by Rebecca - https://history-computer.com/abacus/

[3] Pearson Scott Foresman [Public domain], via Wiki Commons - https://commons.wikimedia.org/wiki/File%3AAstrolabe_(PSF).png

[4] Analytical Engine - https://en.wikipedia.org/wiki/Analytical_Engine

[5] Picture by Ing. Richard Hilber - Self-photographed, Public Domain, https://commons.wikimedia.org/w/index.php?curid=8724964